94CREATIONS5

Publisher
Adriena Dame

Editors
Charlene Luck
Angela Jackson-Brown
Laura Caitlin Davis
Julia Crittendon
Nuray Yasalanyar
Erin Pike
Amy Jackson

Student Editors
Patricia Charron
Brittany Tracy
Morgan Payne
Marcade White
Myranda Vanover

94 Creations, founded in 2007 and relaunched in 2012,
is a literary journal committed to celebrating previously
unpublished fiction, creative nonfiction, drama, poetry, and whatnot.
The editorial team exercises creative license to vary the overall
presentation of this book from issue to issue, and is committed to
publishing a collection of work at least once a year.

94 Creations
www.94creations.com

978-0-9857056-3-3

94 CREATIONS 5

PUBLISHER'S NOTE

94 Creations is a print literary journal committed to publishing an eclectic assortment of outstanding fiction, creative nonfiction, poetry, drama, and art by both emerging and established writers and artists. We welcome the gritty, offbeat, marvelous works often overlooked in mainstream publishing venues, as well as those works that create an authentic experience within the framework of more conventional literary landscapes. We are also interested in celebrating diversity, and are eager to attract the attention of exceptional writers of beautifully varied backgrounds.

My ninety-four-year-old grandmother, Narvelle Jasmine Alexander Littleton (1913-2007), was a significant inspiring force behind the founding of this publication. She was an unsung seamstress, master cook, interior designer, gardener, teacher, peace keeper, wisdom giver, and had a way of making a way out of no way. I am proud to be a part of the legacy she helped to forge.

I am also thankful for the phenomenal editors, whose love, respect, friendship, time, energy, and teamwork have made this issue possible. Effusive thanks to Laura, for diligently transitioning into her forthcoming role as co-managing editor of the journal; to Char, for her willingness to do whatever is needed to get the job done, and for simultaneously contributing her time and energy to *94 Creations and* the debut issue of *Iris Brown Lit Mag*; to Angela, for hanging in here with us while in the throes of touring her first novel, *Drinking from a Bitter Cup*; to Erin, for helping us to transition into an official nonprofit while working on an MFA in writing studies; to Julia and Nuray for their continued enthusiasm and support; to Amy for joining the team and diving in with oodles of bright ideas; and to our Spalding BFA in Writing student editors for their outstanding proofreading skills.

I believe that *every* submission is valuable, tangible, inspiring evidence that writers are out there, daring to share their creations at the risk of rejection, and at the risk of acceptance. Thus, my gratitude for all of the artists whose creative works appear herein, and all of the artists who sought, but did not achieve, publication with us this time around, is boundless.

Thank you for your interest in *94 Creations*. We look forward to your readership for many issues to come.

~ Adriena Dame, Publisher

EDITORIAL TEAM

ADRIENA DAME, author of *The Moo: Stories and a Novella* and publisher of *Iris Brown Lit Mag*, is a professor of undergraduate creative writing courses at Spalding University, and a board member for Louisville Literary Arts, Kentucky Foundation for Women, and Generation iSpeak. She also designs SOSAJI! Socks and Damejoyas jewelry art, and teaches English as a Second Language.

LAURA CAITLIN DAVIS is a student in Spalding University's low-residency MFA in Writing Program, and holds a BA in Anthropology from the University of Louisville. She has worked as an editor for several years. Her stories appear in The Heartland Review and The One Million Stories Project. On her wrist, she sports a black and purple tattoo she calls her "perpetual purple prompt." It reads Ecrivez, a French word that essentially means, "Dude, you better write!"

CHARLENE LUCK is a fiction writer from the Greater Detroit Area. She is a graduate of the University of Michigan's MFA in prose program, where she completed her thesis, a collection of short stories titled "In Your Houses." Her short story, "Grey Herons," was a finalist in the Glimmer Train Stories Summer Short-Short Fiction Contest 2007. She lives in Louisville, Kentucky with her husband, Jeff, and three cats: Manny, Mike, and Cheszwyck.

ANGELA JACKSON-BROWN is the author of *Drinking From a Bitter Cup*, published in 2014 by WiDo Press, is a poet and writer residing in Indianapolis, Indiana. She is an English professor at Ball State University and a graduate of the Spalding University's low-residency MFA in Writing Program. Her work appears in *Pet Milk*, *The Louisville Review*, *New Southerner Literary Magazine*, *94 Creations* and *Muscadine Lines: A Southern Journal*. Her short story, "Something in the Wash," was awarded the 2009 fiction prize by *New Southerner Literary Magazine* and was nominated for a Pushcart Prize in Fiction.

JULIA CRITTENDON is the publisher of *Metamorphosis: Inspirational Stories of Women Living with Alopecia* (her success story is featured in the December/January 2012 issue of *Ebony Magazine*). A woman of many hats, she is co-founder of SOSAJI!, an emerging, private-label sock company; she works as a personal trainer, fitness coach, and phlebotomist; and she is the director of Generation iSpeak, a youth-centered non-profit organization designed to facilitate learning and exploration in the areas of literacy, arts, and education.

ERIN PIKE is an attorney by day and a fiction writer by night. Born and raised in Louisville, Kentucky, Erin attended the University of Louisville, where she received a BA in Philosophy and graduated with honors. She went on to receive her JD from the University of Louisville Brandeis School of Law, after which she spent several years writing and researching for judges in her state's highest courts. Erin now spends her free time writing novel-length fiction for young adults. She is currently a student in the MFA in Writing For Children and Young Adults program at Vermont College of Fine Arts.

AMY JACKSON is a fiction writer who grew up in southeastern Kentucky and wandered around Providence, Rhode Island and San Francisco before finally heeding the call to come back to the South. She holds an MA in English from the University of Kentucky and wrote her thesis on Lewis Carroll and the relationship between writer and reader. Amy currently lives in Louisville, Kentucky with her dog Lucky and is working on her first novel.

CONTENTS

POETRY CONTEST

14   TENEICE DURRANT . GUEST POETRY EDITOR
         Spared
            Daddy's Girl

18   ANNA GOODSON . WINNER
         In the Kitchen My Mother
            The Space Left Behind/Creates a Space Left to Fill
            Thalassophobia

24   KAREN GEORGE . 1ST RUNNER UP
         In River Dreams I'm Always Going Under
         Your Handwriting
            Past Life Flash at Feast of The Flowering
         Moon, Chillicothe, Ohio

30   MOLLY FULLER . 2ND RUNNER UP
         Girl, Falling From Sky
            A Story About Ophelia
            Low, In the Rain

MORE FABULOUS WORKS

34   MONETA GOLDSMITH . Poetry
         An Hour is a Tear, so Stop Counting

38   RACHAEL ARMSTRONG . Fiction
         Last Chance Aloha

50   ELIZABETH FILIATREAU . Fiction
         Release

78   **KIMBERLY CRUM** . Creative Nonfiction
          Slouching Toward Self-Actualization

92   **FREDERICK POLLACK** . Poetry
          Cares of a Dragon
          The Revolt of the Angels

98   **RENE MULLEN** . Fiction
          The Devil Inside

104   **MARIUS SURLEAC** . Poetry
          Bipolar
          Gazers

108   **JOHN SINDELL** . Fiction
          A Man Forbid

126   **MAURICE RUFFIN** . Fiction
          Heroes and Villains

144   **LORETTA WALKER** . Poetry
          How to Fight Like a Girl
          A Letter to the Woman in the Black
          Dress Standing Near the Window

94 Creations Poetry Contest Editor

TENEICE DURRANT is the managing editor of Winged City Chapbook Press and co-founder and poetry editor for *Blood Lotus: an online literary journal*. She is an advocate for chapbooks of all genres, and is the author of three poetry chapbooks: *Flame Above Flame* (2006), *The Goldilocks Complex* (2009), and *Burden of Solace* (2012). Teneice is a proud graduate of Spalding University's MFA in Writing Program, and The University of Toledo's MA in English Literature program. She recently won the 2013 Kudzu Poetry Prize for her poem "Nectar."

SPARED

What if instead of turning, or
tripping, then flaking into a coarse
pillar, Lot's wife pressed on,
the backs of her daughters' heads
shining like lodestars, their amber
or flax hair, come loose from haste,
lit by a thousand tiny stars
making their way towards sin. What if
her virgin children, motherless in a brutal land
was more frightening, just slightly more
frightening than never seeing him,
the one who helped carry her
baskets when Lot couldn't be found.
What if verses later, after whispering,
"Don't worry, it's not incest, just
fornication," into hungover ears,
she ran back to the ridge above Sodom,
stood paralyzed, only her eyes searching,
searching.

DADDY'S GIRL

Everyone thinks of the birth
first, the split from my father's
head, full-grown, yes
even *there*. No mother's rope
to tether me, no midwife
to extract me, no swaddle, no milk.
I already know everything about combat.
Nike and I rub olive oil into battle-tired
muscles, victory lips
twitching. We kick stones
at the graveyard of this war,
masturbate over the casualties
of the next. I break every man
I hold, only some on purpose. Even
proud Zeus winces, tells me
it wasn't the pounding of my
shield that drove him mad,
but Metis and I,

whispering.

ANNA E. GOODSON studies creative writing and music performance at Michigan State University Honors College. She works with writers Diane Wakoski, Marcia Aldrich, and Ray Paris. Her work appears in *Open Palms Print*, and she is the winner of the 2013 Live Lit at Michigan State and Runner Up for 2013 RCAH Poetry Contest at Michigan State, judged by poet Carl Phillips.

IN THE KITCHEN MY MOTHER

In the kitchen my mother cooks pasties,
cracks eggs and picks out the gold,
eats it. Outside, the lightning
is paler than my mother's forearms, all
the little red hairs of electricity foaming
from the current. The edge of where
the lightning splits the sky like a marbled
counter spattered with flour & vinegar.
In the kitchen my mother smears lard
on a sheet of iron and hums;
outside there is an egg left by a mother
swan, the baby squirming inside. She will
ask me to throw it in the river, to get rid
of it, will not be able to watch the egg
crack against the surface of the lake,
the water & gold frothing, the tiny
pachyderm falling silently like a drop
of sweat from her brow, will not
like the idea of some fish or turtle,
some deep aquatic animal, eating
the not-yet-swan raw.

THE SPACE LEFT BEHIND/ CREATES A SPACE LEFT TO FILL

Imagine the space left when
Icarus parted the sea like a bullet
creating space inside flesh. Did Daedalus
begin to think of that space as belonging
to him? Daedalus watching the sea opening
and closing to fit his daughter –
remembering how, as a child, he'd sit
on his back porch like day-old milk,
the rings left inside the bottle, measuring
empty space now.

*

There's no adjective for a cut
tree, just my mother sobbing at
the stump left behind. Like the rings
when my father left the coffee pot
on old newsprint/ my father with his feather-beard
and glasses made of sea bones. Or when I lost
my hair, when I was thin/ sharper
than a rhombus, my mother pulling
out thick strands. She said it was
easy, like shucking corn – leaving behind
the nub of a scalp like a worm curled
into the space left behind where a
niblet fell out.

*

Time is just measuring space.
The space between the finger & the ring
on the finger of the boy I lost when I was Icarus.
The space between my fingers and the fingers of
the boy I kept when I was the child that lived.
Rings of light from the moon drawing
ripples across his hair.
The space left to paint on both
sides – an incomplete painting on one,
the first strokes of a new painting
on the other.

*

Meanwhile the leaves gather on
one side of the bridge I am leaning over,
watching these leaves spread out like
an impressionist painting dissolving
sideways.

THALASSOPHOBIA

When he asks if I love him,
he asks for a word that is, even after months,
as startling as looking into a tidal pool
& seeing a fish peering from a spill
of red algae.
It is a movement of the tongue
like the part of the wave that is
just behind the foam,
that is pulled by the breaking of the water
but does not itself fold.
It is my fear of the sea,
of limitlessness,
eggs of a fish
hidden in coral
burnt by the pressure.
And meanwhile, in the susurrus of a language
the water can promise will never be ours,
the waves keep breaking to divide
again, again, again.

94 Creations Poetry Contest 1st Runner Up

KAREN GEORGE is the author of *Into the Heartland* (Finishing Line Press, 2011) and *Inner Passage* (Red Bird Chapbooks, 2014). Her work also appears in *Memoir*, *Tupelo Press 30/30* Website, *Louisville Review, Permafrost, Cortland Review,* and *Wind.* She has been awarded grants from The Kentucky Foundation for Women and The Kentucky Arts Council, is a graduate of Spalding University's low-residency MFA in Writing Program, and she reviews poetry at *Poetry Matters.*

IN RIVER DREAMS I'M ALWAYS GOING UNDER

Brakes fail, the bridge unbuckles
or climbs higher, higher
and when I reach
the summit, no way down
but to nosedive toward the shine.

No time to eject before impact,
metal collapses in,
the crush-suck catapults me
into cold dark plush
heavy on my head.

O, the urge to rise,
my kicks thick as the muck,
the musk metallic like blood,
chestache of lungs longing
until light tendrils down.

Clouds of sediment churn
when I frog-kick off the bottom,
arms overhead,
body a bullet.

O, the breakthrough.
Nails of my fingers
pierce the river skin, scrim
that hems air.

The dream ends
before I thrash my arms,
throw my voice across water
to a triangle in the inlet,
the boat that will turn for me.

YOUR HANDWRITING

As the anniversary of your death nears,
I feel the pull to see your handwriting, hold

papers you pressed pens against, read
your words, the ways you formed letters

in journals, notes on beloved books,
prayers you wrote.

You braid cursive with printed
letters that slant like calligraphy.

Your *P* in *Peace* plump as a down pillow,
and like Emily, your capitalization never standard.

Your *n* mimics a *u*.
When a word begins with *d*,

as in *dwell*, you form a flat, straight staff
but when at word's end, as in *surround*,

the staff's fat as a baseball bat, and instead of lilting
right, it leans left as if to shield letters beneath it.

Sometimes you break words—
stre tch, *Kind ness*, *brea the*.

I mouth them, touch their wings and sutures. You
lean near, and I divine the deep murmur of your voice.

PAST LIFE FLASH AT FEAST OF THE FLOWERING MOON, CHILLICOTHE, OHIO

I inhale sage smoke, feel grass blades tickle, the cool May
ground rumble with the Native American dance—leap and
lunge of feathered headdresses, shirts, capes, and aprons
adorned with beads, fringe, and ribbons

my vision curls closed like the end chamber of a
kaleidoscope rotates, spirals to a point of no light, a silent
scene appears as on a movie screen, swatches of blurred
motion focuses to a girl behind an Indian on a horse, flanks
wet, buckskin pants, a calico dress, her open mouth, the
scream slams into my chest, smothered by the man's
knotted back, tang of dried mud and sweat, tips of his hair
lash my cheeks, hooves pound the ground, the snort of
nostrils, I taste dust and blood, hooves hair mud sweat
knots buckskin calico blur

my vision unfurls into a kaleidoscope of leap and lunge—
beads, fringe, ribbons, feathers—cool May ground rumbles,
grass blades tickle, I inhale sage smoke.

94 Creations Poetry Contest 2nd Runner Up

MOLLY FULLER is a Visiting Assistant Professor of English at Marshall University, where she teaches writing. She holds a BSJ in Journalism and an MA in English from Ohio University, and an MFA in Fiction from Sarah Lawrence College. She is the author of three chapbooks, *The Neighborhood Psycho Dreams of Love, Tender the Body,* and *All My Loves* (forthcoming). Her prose poems and micro fiction appear in *Hot Metal Bridge, Potomac, Crack the Spine, Calliope,* and *Union Station Magazine.*

GIRL, FALLING FROM SKY

She tumbles beautifully, ecstatically, through this blank canvas day. Careening headlong, head strong, pulled like stars fall to earth, like water flows down, the weight of gravity heavy upon her.

Her arms reach up. Toward the blue sky that hangs, fixed there above her streaming hair, just out of fingertip reaching. The sun, hot on her limbs, on her face, dazzles her eyes like lightning as she falls toward a rush of silver water that will clasp her body.

The desire to feel it all at once overwhelms her. She hears the rustle of the river below, sees the curls of white clouds that will cross the sun, intuits the moon beyond the horizon, a cold white face looking down at her as she plunges into iciness. It is unbearable and joyful as her mouth clutches the water and her arms break the surface. Suddenly she wants to breathe. Breathe.

A STORY ABOUT OPHELIA

She is wet. Her hair will not dry. She twists the strands around and around in her palms, but the hair keeps stretching. Like fishing line. Like taffy. She stands knee-deep in the water. Her feet are covered in silt. She bends toward her toes to see them better, but she only succeeds in getting the tip of her nose wet. This makes her laugh. This laughter is a lovely sound. We all run to hear it. We want to join her. But what if we all get tangled in hair? What if she were to drown?

LOW, IN THE RAIN

Ponytailed, knee-socked, silk-pantied pleasure—my apocryphal, tumultuous Lolita. Your rosy-cheeked complicity in this soiled charade is beautiful, voluptuous. Lips to lips, breasts to breasts, kneeling by the side of the wistful motel pool. Here an amusing moody agony in your ruffled, bow-trimmed bikini—chauffeuring me feelingless through these corporeal transactions. Dim light shines from underwater portholes, becomes shadowed loopholes for exploration, evocation, my sinking in to saturated, blue-tinged delight. Breathless, shipwrecked, I rest my cheek on your peach-fuzzed thighs. The blood hums tenderly in my temples as picnickers in the distance are illuminated by lightning.

MONETA GOLDSMITH is a writer, teacher, and former poetry editor of *The Northridge Review*. His works appear in *Sparkle & Blink, Apiary Magazine,* and *East Jasmine Review,* among others.

AN HOUR IS A TEAR, SO STOP COUNTING

Writer wants to sing
lullabies to onions
& ice cream cones.
But nothing good
ever happened
to anyone who
woke up & said:

'I am going to write
something great today!'

Sometimes writer will get discouraged
and open up to a book of
another writer—
a writer who uses phrases like:

'rogue on the run'
or
'rolling infinitely in the virgin spaces,'
or else (about the darkness),
'irksome and profound.'

then writer will get discouraged
all over again
or find some new purpose
or find a way to work those
phrases into a poem of his own.

Writer still remembers whistling melodies

somewhat deliberately and loud.

So loud writer's melodies might have
reached the castles in Spain
if writer had kept up with it;
so loud writer's melodies
would have been thrown out
of castles for bad behavior.
No small feat in Spain.

Onions, peppers, chula sauce,
writer wants them.

A 'short talk'
given by Gertrude Stein:

well, look at that.
it's 9:30 in the evening!
the day is over.
I had no idea!

Writer remembers looking at a magnolia
tree and thinking of a sunflower. Thinking:

I bet Luxembourg gardens were jealous
of Kew gardens after Virginia Woolf showed up.

Thinking
of all the ways a sunflower has of loving light—

there's dappled light, mobled
and diaphanous light.

Let's see, there is

cold and heavy,
dark and mysterious,
there is a light that is
'irksome and profound'
(writer's favorite)

Writer wants to be
a rogue on the run, dark and mysterious,
rolling infinitely
in the virgin spaces.
…irksome and profound.

Writer thinks:
of all the ways the sunflower has of loving
light, there is still no way to alleviate
thirst, mystery, the hunger that sometimes swells
the size and texture of eternity,
pestilence, pain.

Writer dreams of too many castles in Spain
and also, not enough.

Writer has a way of looking at the magnolia
trees longer than he probably should.

RACHAEL ARMSTRONG earned her MFA in Creative Writing from the University of Washington and is co-founder and fiction editor of the independent literary journal *Pacifica Literary Review*. Her work appears in Florida Atlantic University's literary journal, *Coastlines, Squalorly Magazine*, and is forthcoming in *Hobart*. She is currently writing a novel.

LAST CHANCE ALOHA

This story is an intimate engagement piece based on "Beverly Home" by Denis Johnson.

Every now and then in the mornings I liked to visit the greenhouse at the rehabilitation center next door, a large off-white building with a glass ceiling where the air was mollifying and warm, like the kind of sex I wanted. During this time there was a lovely woman with short dark hair and a pale complexion who watered the plants. I got the feeling I bothered her, mostly because, in my nervousness, all I could think to talk about was myself. I asked her if she'd like to go out with me, and she told me she had a complicated ailment that prevented her from spending much time socially. I wondered about this, though she told me, if I wanted to, I could come back and see her there. I sensed she was too mature for me, but I also knew right away that I wanted to come back. Sometimes there were ropes of light in the sky hovering so low it seemed I could have raised my arms to climb them—avenues to a new universe—the silky light portending a fantastic, benevolent era.

I felt like one of the animals I cared for during that time. I'd found a job because my substance-free philosophy determined I be self-sustainable. My probation officer seemed to think it was a happy thing, because it was a necessary thing. And when I told people what I was doing —my family back home, and so on—they seemed happy, too.

It was my former M.O. to act with scavenger-like opportunism, and it hadn't led me anywhere worthwhile. In a way, working at the animal clinic was my last chance "to get back on track," a phrase I heard pretty frequently in those days. Perhaps when you hear the word *Aloha* you think of islands and vacation—people wandering sandy beaches drowning their livers with Mai Tais and tanning lotion. Or you think of girls wearing plump purple leis and grass skirts, greeting you. But *Aloha* is meant to conjure the elemental: affection, love, peace and mercy. I frequently lay awake at night, thinking about mercy. The clinic was a destination for animals injured or diseased beyond the point of repair, a sort of hospice. In the center of the building was an outdoor area with several large tanks for monk seals, and I liked to imagine how it would look like a giant target if seen from the sky.

Not all of our patients at *Aloha Veterinary Clinic* were dying. Some were healthy but mangled. Some had brain complications that bent their necks at severe angles and drew their lips into horrifying grins. Others seemed okay when you first met them, but ended up having tumors the size of basketballs hidden under their flippers, for example. It made God seem careless. There was a bat with a gland disorder that caused her to swell to three times the normal size. Her name was Roberta. Each day someone wiped her down with a wet rag and then she sat mostly motionless, propped upright in her cage like a stuffed Halloween doll. Her claws were about a foot long. Her head like a big wedge of cantaloupe. You and I don't see these disorders unless our pets end up with them, in which case we have them put down.

This was a part-time affair. I wasn't qualified to do much more than comfort the animals: stroke them and cuddle them, scratch them in the places they couldn't reach, and alleviate their suffering with my attentive presence. I also kept the coffee going in the treatment room. And it was indirectly my job to keep morale up when moods were bleak. The veterinarian employed at this facility was a young woman named Carla. You could tell things in her life hadn't often worked out well because when one of the animals died she became deeply depressed and stayed for a long time in her office, under her desk with a blanket over her face. I would go in and sit with her while the technicians dropped the dead animal into a plastic bag and locked it away into the freezer, where it would be kept until collected by animal control. She would say things to me like, "This is what I get for dreaming," then roll over, turning away.

(In the tank out back a seal barking like, "Yup, yup, yup...")

I would sit on the floor next to her and pull my fingers through her hair. She was a different person at night, but who isn't? Meanwhile, the employees rushed through the halls with the deceased animal in their arms. Most of them were women, and the animals would be held pillowed against their breasts, but always their frightened eyes made me think of the soft light of stars, far away.

There was one young man who worked there, and he walked the curved halls with a lost expression similar to mine. But his eccentricity was more obvious, which, perhaps, is why no one ever questioned the two of us about our personal lives, or tried to initiate after-hours contact. There's oppression in knowing too much of one's troubles. His mother had recently died, and his girlfriend too. Both tragically. He was only twenty-three. I think he slept on the sofa-bed of one of the older women, our secretary at the clinic. His face had two separate, sporadic ways of twitching: occasionally his eye, sometimes the corner of his mouth. He hummed rakishly all day and smoked pot in the alley outside, but I liked him, because he didn't try to pretend.

When work ended at two p.m. I strolled the lonely beaches. The highway running parallel to the coast was often lined with rental cars, like ants in a row. They went from one famous beach to another, but they left ours alone.

One day, walking high up on the shore where the trees and wild scrub grew, I was kicking through the seaweed and looking for drift seeds, which I liked to polish and keep for good luck. Beyond the veil of vegetation were the backyards of dozens of small homes. A quiet neighborhood. Eventually I could hear the quick cadence of a running shower, and then the spangled sound of water falling on stone. I stopped and raised my head. Peering through the trees, I saw a woman standing in the early afternoon sunshine beneath a tall shower with a bright copper nozzle. She was nude, so it took me a moment to realize that it was the woman who worked at the rehabilitation center, the one I'd spoken to in the greenhouse. Her skin reflected a warm light that broke through the branches and covered me in a quilted pattern. She had her arms held up and was catching the water as it fell into her cupped palms; I couldn't at first see her nipples. Then she dropped her hands and, like an imaginary chalice had fallen, water streamed down her small face, her pale nipples, and her ingenious stomach in luminous waves.

She bathed unconsciously, oblivious to exposure. She wasn't what you might call indulgent about it, but there was sensuality in her movements. She sang to herself, a bewitching sound, though her words weren't perceptible. I was aroused. How could this have fallen into my lap, if it wasn't something like fate?

I burrowed down into the growth. The woman lifted her face up to the sky and the water dripped from her dark hair. It streamed around her ears and stuck to her face and neck in pretty wet hollows that I wanted to kiss. I was in a trance, every muscle in my body poised to spring. I thought if I was a man I might've raped her; my desires were too furtive for that. When she reached to turn off the water I wanted to cry out. She took a towel from the ground and dried off, shaking her hair, then stepped into denim shorts and flip flops and walked under a trellis of alert ylang-ylang covering the back patio of her house, to where I could no longer see her.

I was wild and anxious. I had been experiencing a thrilling head rush, and I wasn't ready for it to end. Creeping more deeply into the brush I could make out a window on the left side of the house, and I crept along until I was quite close to it. From there I could see into her living room. After a minute or so she walked in wearing a bra and exercise shorts with a purple mat under her arm, which she unrolled on the floor. She stretched, seated herself, and began executing hand and body motions which I thought might be yoga, but then perhaps were slower, more on-the-spot. At different intervals she would bend over her lithe legs, hug them and exhale, facing down. When she rose again her eyes would be teary and her face flushed.

Then suddenly I had a terrible premonition, like an invisible hand had grazed my cheek, and I turned in time to notice a troop of park rangers marching by, to check on the turtle nests along the beach. I lay flat to the ground and they passed without noticing. I peeked in the window again before I left, but she had gone.

The woman I was dating during this time was the veterinarian who I worked for. I knew she wasn't seeing me exclusively—this was only one point of contention—but she told me I was the only woman she was seeing and that might have been true. Being awash in the energy of her frenetic off-duty personas often left me exhausted. She "channeled" what she referred to as "spirits," and she frequently delivered cryptic messages to me about my life and what lay in my future. (Yet there were often times days later when, like encountering a dream or an enchantment, I'd confront a situation she had exactly foretold.) Carla had a tough, articulated way of holding herself that suggested internal ferocity, and gray eyes full of mystery and panache. Beyond this, something about her was extremely sad. When we made love I had to be careful to keep my eyes moving, as I couldn't bear to acknowledge the depth of her pain, lest I be compelled to make some sort of vow. I could never truly reach her: perched as she was over some distant netherworld she would always be haunted by. But she had a sensitive, Samaritan soul, and she was wise.

Certainly she was touched. I felt like I could be open with her, except for as related to one thing.

It was late in the cyclone season, and the last big storms were just coming on. The gusts of sand on the beach made it easy for me to disappear as I drifted along and edged into the trees behind the house of the woman I'd become so very infatuated with. I knew I should have simply visited the greenhouse like she'd suggested. Maybe something could have slowly developed between us. But the situation was already far too developed for that, and I was desperate.

I felt I knew her intimately. I liked spending time with her,even though I knew that I was being a pervert. Watching her shower had become the most pleasurable part of my routine. The four days became the focal point of my entire existence. She would perform her spellbinding ablutions, and I would watch from the brush, and then she would go inside, and I would slink to her living room window like a bandit or a cat, to catch her emerge clean and radiant to begin her exercises, which I'd never decoded but had begun to suspect were spiritual in their intent. Sometimes people would dart past on the beach, so I had to be cautious, but over time I could feel myself becoming fearless in the sort of way that usually led to trouble for me.

On Thursdays at the Aloha Clinic we took all the birds outside. It was cramped for them in the cages, and they grew pitiful and dreary after too many days without being exercised. None were fit for the wild: some were missing wings, others, like two pheasants, had been caught by dogs and sustained injuries that didn't allow them to take more than a few wobbly steps at a time. Outside however, the birds revitalized. They shook out their feathers and made radiant shrieks and calls to one another. There was a social hierarchy among them, and while in the windowless clinic they fussily taunted each other, outside they sung affectionately and purred. A couple of them could hold themselves on a perch for an hour or two, but most eventually shuffled together into an ellipse over the ground, where they nibbled the tips of grass until we brought them back inside. What I didn't feel able to express was how normal it was for me to be there, among them, displaced.

Most Sundays Carla and I had dinner and made love, the former usually take-out from local Teriyaki joints, because neither of us liked to cook. I decided that I would enact a betrayal and spend a full Sunday at the woman's house instead of with Carla. I was terrifically excited with the possibilities of what I could see. I knew she lived alone. She led a disciplined life, each week adhering to a prodigious schedule of work, exercise, reading, and study. I assumed she was an academic performing research at the greenhouse. I'd hoped she would swim, too, because she lived right alongside the ocean, but if she did it must have been early in the morning when I wasn't there. I came to enjoy watching her read or fold her laundry just as much as I first enjoyed watching her shower. I'd come very close several times to tapping my long watching fingers against the windowpane, but the possibility of being prohibited from ever seeing her again clutched me with a profound panic, and I never followed through.

More than anything, I wanted to see this woman please herself sexually. It seemed bound to happen if I waited with her long enough. In other words, if I came on Sunday.

I woke at six in the morning from a dreamless sleep and freed myself from the web of blankets in Carla's bed. She moaned, rolling over. In the kitchen I made coffee and watched the sky spread with light, the little waves in her swimming pool twinkling like diamonds had rained down during the night. I took a shower and let myself out of the house before Carla woke up.

It was hard for me to live sober because I would see a morning like this one and feel really excited about it in a way I used to only be able to express by getting hammered. My plan for that day had been to walk to her house, stake out a good position in the trees. But from a tug in my gut I turned in the opposite direction and began walking toward the animal clinic. There would be some employees there, feeding and tidying up the animal cages, and Carla would come by for one or two hours in the afternoon.

When I got to the clinic I didn't walk inside but continued on, and then I was standing in front of the greenhouse, staring up at the paint peeling from its exterior. When I walked in, the air that rushed over me was like muttering voices, and I could see from across the long room that the woman was indeed there, watering the plants. When I came up behind her she lowered the hose and spun around, dazedly, then remembering, she said hello and gestured for me to follow her.

Inside a tiny office near the back of the building there was a desk crowded with papers and a very old computer. A swivel chair waited nearby. On the chair was a shoebox, lined with toilet paper, and partly swaddled inside of it was a small bird, a sand-piper, not moving.

"I found it on the beach outside of my house this morning, after my swim," she said.

I searched her face for hidden meanings, but could find none.

The sandpiper looked as if its neck was broken, and as if it were already dead, but on closer inspection it appeared that the pupil was oscillating swiftly between opening to light and closing finally to darkness--the firings of a neurological system. I held the box as she gathered her things, and we walked across the street together to the clinic. The air was electrical. I had a key to the back door, and as I prepared to unlock I noticed that some of the employees were gathered across the beach. They were smoking cigarettes and pointing at the sky. The woman placed her hand gently on my lower back, steadying me down even to my electrons, and we walked toward them in what was the most joyous moment of my life.

This was my last chance, really; where I'd erred before was behind me now. I cupped my hand over the sandpiper to give it warmth, like incubating an egg.

Far offshore and hovering above the ocean was a large thunderhead, the largest I'd ever seen. It was the cloud that plumes up after a nuclear bomb and it was scudding our way, crackling with lightning and thunder. The sound in the distance arrived to us like *pssst*, static on the airwaves. I thought of how we would need to find shelter, a basic thing, and how many of us would find it there in the clinic. We would protect the animals. It made me feel happy for us, because sometimes we did the right thing.

I didn't know where I'd end up, maybe Carla did and it was truly grim, but the young man with the twitch started to hum, and as rain began sprinkling down on us we turned as a group or a herd or a pack and walked toward Aloha, leaning into the wind. Below the wind there was another frequency like the distant blowing of a horn.

Who awaits us?

What a bunch of freaks, I thought, myself included. I didn't deserve this luck, but shards of magic were raining from the sky. In the air was a sexy new glow. I'd never imagined, never dreamed for even an instant that there would be a refuge for the likes of us, or that I would ever be forgiven. But in the midst of disaster, there we all were, closer than ever.

ELIZABETH FILIATREAU has had a hand in grant writing, newspaper editing, and publishing as a guest columnist in the Courier-Journal. After years of following other people's dreams, she is in pursuit of her own brand of happiness, which includes becoming a successful writer. She has two children and two grandchildren, and she lives in Louisville, Kentucky with her dogs, Mabel and Zoey Doodle, who only interrupt her writing when it interferes with their suppertime.

RELEASE

Jen

Jen's hand was shaking as she hit the Print icon on her computer screen. On the desk in front of her, the printer cartridge slid back and forth across the page, creating an airline ticket from Cody to Louisville, creating a clear exit strategy from life as she knew it.

She looked around the bedroom, where she now slept alone every night. Aside from the picture of her parents on her bedside table and the stack of books next to the bed, there was nothing of her in this room. It was just another in a series of rooms that she briefly inhabited while she followed Tucker from one fantasy to the next.

As if to echo her thoughts, the television in the living room was reporting a story about bears being caged in Yellowstone, and she was struck by the absurdity of finding herself living in a place where the local news was about bears.

Thinking about bears, she pushed away from the desk and walked to the window. She and Tucker called it the Magic Window because they never knew what they were going to see when they opened the blinds. One morning she heard a sniffling sound and looked out to see a grizzly under the crabapple tree, scarfing down the fallen crabapples and standing up on its hind legs to knock more of them to the ground. Tucker had pointed out bear scat under the tree, but somehow she hadn't fully made the connection that scat equals bear.

When they first moved to Wapiti, halfway between Cody and the east entrance to Yellowstone Park, she looked out the Magic Window early one morning to see the golden valley across the highway, where two perfectly straight lines of cows stood facing each other, as if they were waiting for the first strains of a fiddle so they could bow to their partners and do-si-do. She called Tucker to the window, tickled by her imagined cow dance. He was so amused by her naiveté that he was sorry to have to tell her they were cattle, not cows (cows are female bovines that have had a calf, and cattle is plural of both male and female), and that they were lined up because that's where the rancher's machinery had laid down their feed.

On another occasion, she was drawn to the window by the thundering of hooves and looked out to see an endless parade of trail horses running right down the center of the highway, with honest-to-god cowboys moving them from their mountain pastures to the resorts nearer town for tourist season.

Mostly what she saw from that window, what made it truly magical to her, was the ever-changing face of the Absaroka Range. The mountains were sometimes beige and gray, shrouded in fog or smoke from the wildfires. Or they were sparkling sun on ice. Look again and they were a pastel worthy of Monet, all soft blues, lavenders and pinks. Or, with a swift change of God's palette, they were gold and red, standing harshly against a brilliant blue sky. With time, she learned to see the elk and antelope by allowing her eyes to go unfocused until a movement gave her a place to hone in.

Looking at them now, she realized that she had never, in her forty years of life on this earth, understood the word majestic until she got to know the mountains. And she would miss them, along with the sharp smell of sage and cedar and the spare and honest way of the people who lived in this high desert country.

She knew she would miss Tucker, too. But if she was honest with herself, the Tucker she had fallen in love with and married had gone missing some time back, and the occasional glimpses she caught of that Tucker were not enough to sustain her, not enough to balance out all the rest of him. Sadder yet, the sassy Jen who had fallen in love with Tucker and was always onboard with his adventures was gone too. She had met the bogey man and his name was Bipolar Disorder. Tucker carried what Jen called the sneaky bastard into their home every day and she had to be vigilant for both of them; because no matter how consistently he showed up, Tucker never recognized him. Jen felt like a little police force, here to serve and protect.

Jen left the window, took the ticket from the printer tray, folded it in thirds and hid it under her pillow. She then sat down on the bed feeling the heaviness of what she was doing. Although she tried to envision a life without Tucker, she could never get past stepping off the airplane in Louisville.

In a way, she was going full-circle. Louisville was where she had met Tucker, where they'd lived the biggest part of their marriage, where they'd been happiest. And she knew she would see him everywhere. But Louisville was also where she was born, where she would have the support of her huge extended family and life-long friends as she tried to figure out how to be in the world without Tucker.

Jen moved to the dresser and the portable phone. As she picked it up, she looked at herself in the mirror. She didn't see the woman with the dark, glossy hair and rosy complexion that her friends coveted. She didn't see the long legs and trim waist. She saw the old hag that hid from others, the one with the age in her eyes and the permanently downturned lips. She saw the slumped shoulders that sheltered her horrible angry heart.

Turning her back on that woman, Jen called Tucker's cell phone, knowing that he wouldn't answer. Trying to sound as normal as possible, she left a message asking that he try to get home as soon as he could tonight, that she had something she needed to talk over with him.

"Tucker," she said into the phone, "Please—this time—call me if you're going to be late."

Tucker

Tucker bounced along the gravel road that led out of the Wild Mustang Sanctuary, where he had spent the morning with his boss, Marshall, and a particularly skittish pinto mare. He loved his work at the sanctuary, loved especially the moment when a horse's fear gave way to trust and he was rewarded with a handful of warm, velvet breath.

He loved that job even more than he hated his job at the Flying J, where he catered to a bunch of spoiled tourists. *Jen's working two jobs,* Tucker always thought. *Well three if you count the book-keeping she does on the side. Better just suck it up.* Thinking of Jen reminded him that he had missed a call from her that morning, but he was running late so he made a mental note to call her once he got to the bar.

The bar of the Flying J Resort was a popular tourist watering hole. It was a long slab of polished wood that was said to have come from the original bar in Cody and to have accommodated the elbows of Buffalo Bill himself. The storied bar boasted a wagon-wheel chandelier that hung by chains from the vaulted wooden ceiling, cozy booths with red leather and nail-head upholstery and a gallery of mounted heads of buffalo, moose and mountain goat. A bear-skin rug in front of the summer cold fireplace completed the décor.

Just as Tucker was sliding behind the bar, Bob, a tourist with a fly-fishing group from Australia, made his usual obnoxious entrance, patting various patrons on the back and throwing "G'day"s around as if he were the Australian Ambassador to the Flying J. He straddled a stool and checked himself out in the mirror that backed the full length of the bar. He greeted Tucker and ordered a "long pull of the ol' amber fluid." Tucker rolled his eyes at Bob's exaggerated Australian slang he pulled .to draw attention to himself. He pulled a draft beer and slid it down the bar. As soon as Bob was sure he had everyone's attention, he twirled his stool around, rested an elbow on the edge of the bar and started recounting his visit to Yellowstone earlier in the day.

"The little sheila that was leading our tour group was quite a looker," he preened," and she was very taken with my accent."

"Well, thank God for your accent then, 'cause she sure as hell wasn't taken by your looks," Tucker interrupted.

"Well, you're no great specimen yourself," Bob shot back.

But this was patently untrue. Tucker was six feet of compelling details. The circumference of his shining blonde curls was creased from his cowboy hat. His eyes beneath the curls were a mood barometer, ranging from hazy turquoise to angry navy. When they were clear and smiling, they were accompanied by twin dimples and a flash of white teeth in a deeply tanned face. He was what Westerners call a long drink of water, rangy and muscular. His hands were large and calloused, his nails bitten to the quick. One minute he was a shy little boy looking up from under his pale eyelashes; the next he was a hard-ass cowboy.

"After the tour," Bob continued, "she took me aside and asked if I'd like to see some of the places they don't usually take tourists." Bob paused and gave a big wink. "Well, as I said, she was a pretty one and I was more than happy to have a little walkabout with her."

Tucker, who was used to being the one telling the stories, was annoyed by this Australian Banty Rooster. He stuck his thumbs under his arm pits, puffed out his chest and started strutting around. He had the guys laughing at Bob now and asked him, "Do you just make this shit up as you go along?"

Ignoring Tucker, Bob said, "She led me to an old logging road and we had quite the hike. After a bit, I started smelling something fishy and asked her what the hell that was. I followed her to a clearing, and there were

Goldilocks's three fucking bears. But the three of 'em were all locked up in a great steel cage, snarling and banging at the bars. I didn't get what the fishy smell had to do with the bears, but she said their shit smells like fish because that's what they eat this time of year. She said the bears had gotten too close to where the tourists were and that's why they'd been trapped."

This story piqued Tucker's interest, even though it was Bob who told it. Tucker had adopted the locals' love/hate relationship with the tourists. So many of them depended on tourism to make a living, but the tourists were ruining the very things they paid all that money to see. To his way of thinking, they should put the tourists in cages and leave the bears alone.

He asked, "So did she say what would happen to the bears?"

"She said the Rangers would take them to a more remote area of the Park."

By the time Bob ended his story, with him bedding the pretty little sheila of course, he had acquired quite a buzz and more than a little bravado.

Bob was still hanging out at the bar when the other tourists had gone off to their rooms. Tucker was wiping down the counter and trying to close up for the night. He'd taken some extra Ritalin to stay awake; maybe he'd taken too many. He was wired and he needed to get home and down some Valium and Seroquel so he could come down and, *Please God,* he thought, get some sleep for a change. Jen would be pissed. She'd accuse him of messing with his medicines; she'd threaten to call his doctor. And she would explain again, as to a dull child, how important it was that he take the pills as prescribed, helpfully reminding him that they were all counted out and sorted in the pill keeper. She had even gone so far as to keep them locked in the safe for a while. *I can't even control my own medication anymore. Next she'll be wiping my ass.*

"You know what would be fucking awesome?" Bob broke into Tucker's mental conversation. "We should go let those bears out of the cage! All we'd have to do is climb up to the top and unlatch it. Can you imagine the park guys when they come to get them? They'll think it's Jesus and the tomb all over again."

"Shit," Bob yammered on, "If I were back in Australia, my mates and I wouldn't dither about. We'd be out there right now pranking those bastards just for shits and gigs."

Tucker's mind would not release the image of the caged bears. It wasn't the bears' fault that people had taken over their habitat. It wasn't their fault that the idiots left their trash all over the place. The bears didn't want to attack people; if the tourists would just wear bear bells like the Rangers suggested, the bears would hear them coming and run away.

Tucker was tired and irritable, hopped up on Ritalin and sick of hearing Bob's bullshit. He had worked himself into a temper about the bears, so he decided to call Bob's bluff. "Okay, *mate*, he said. "Let's go find us some bears."

Bob was not prepared for this turn of events. "Well, um, I don't have a gun, mate. They don't exactly let you bring firearms on a plane for a fly-fishing trip. And our tour bus is leaving for the airport at seven." Making a show of looking at his watch, he said, "That's just a few hours away."

Tucker had his teeth into the idea now and wasn't about to let it go. He looked into Bob's eyes, daring him to back down. "I have a rifle in the truck. And I'll have you back in plenty of time to catch your bus. Just think what a great Wild, Wild West story it'll make when you get back to Australia. Hell, it might even get you laid again."

Bob, held prisoner by his own ego, got into Tucker's beat up Dodge Ram and they headed down the Wapiti Road towards Yellowstone, turned onto the logging road and followed it into the Park. When the road ended, they parked the car. Tucker grabbed the rifle, took two flashlights from the glove box and gave one to Bob. As they headed off into the scrub pines, Tucker thought maybe he was being played. *Shit, he's drunk. He'll never find those bears.* He laughed to himself as he quietly hummed the song from the Fisher-Price radio he had as a kid: *"It's picnic time for teddy bears. The little teddy bears are having a lovely time today. See them, watch them unaware. They never have a care."*

Tucker was about to share this bit of humor with Bob when he smelled rancid fish and heard a huffing sound. He felt the hair on his neck rise. In fact, he felt every nerve ending come alive as he perceived his surroundings with an uncanny clarity. Feeling completely invincible, he strode into the clearing. He was Davy Crockett, King of the Wild Frontier. All fear left him as he approached the trap. He looked into the eyes of the Mama grizzly and felt an immediate kinship with her. It was as if he could hear her fear, frustration, anger and helplessness through her groans and growls. And he knew that language so well.

By this time, BobFromAustralia, as Tucker had come to think of him, had sobered up enough to realize that maybe this wasn't such a great idea; he tried to pull Tucker away from the trap. "C'mon mate, if we're playing chicken, you win. Let's go back to the lodge before we're mistaken for a couple of big fish."

Tucker wouldn't be convinced. It was suddenly imperative that he free the bear and her cubs. Watching them escape would somehow vindicate all the times he found himself locked behind bars that were invisible but no less real. Walking away would be admitting that there was no way out. BobfromAustralia would never understand.

He handed the rifle to Bob. "Go back to the car. I'll be there in a few minutes."

As Bob made his way back to the car, Tucker studied the trap. It was a metal cylinder on wheels with bars on the front. It looked like a sinister version of the playground clay pipe tunnels that had felt so big to him as a child. But to a grizzly bear, it would be claustrophobic and terrifying. Although it wasn't as tall as he expected, it would definitely require some climbing. Since there was nothing else to climb on, Tucker took a deep breath, grabbed onto the bars and shimmied up the front of the trap.

The bears, which had initially retreated to the back of the cage, charged forward and Mama bear swiped at Tucker, slicing his thigh with one of her massive claws. A rush of adrenaline propelled him to the top of the trap. Once there, he stopped to steady himself and exhale the breath he had unconsciously held. Time slowed and his movements took on a slide-show quality as he carefully stood up, grabbed the handle at the top of the bars and lifted. The bars clicked easily into the latch as it locked in the open position. The sound of release echoed through the black and silent clearing.

Mama and her cubs barreled out of the cage and made for the tree line. When the cubs had reached safety, the big grizzly turned and stood on her hind legs. She snapped her massive jaws and threatened a charge. Tucker was mesmerized as she moved her giant head from side to side, ear-to shoulder, her mouth a nightmare of teeth in the weak beam of his flashlight.

As his Ritalin and endorphins wore off, he began to feel the pain of his injury. His situation no longer seemed like a philosophical exercise. He realized—at least for the moment—that he was no Davy Crockett and that he was in some serious shit.

Following standard bear attack protocol, Tucker would have backed slowly away, but since he couldn't do that without falling off the trap, he drew himself to his full height and tried to look as big as possible. In a suspension of time that might have been seconds or hours, the bear dropped to all fours and lumbered off after her cubs.

Tucker unlatched the lock, and lowered the bars. Next, he laid on his stomach, wrapped first his feet and then his hands around the lowered bars, and slid to the ground. He was simultaneously terrified and exhilarated. As he left the clearing, he looked over his shoulder and saw the cage as a giant pill bottle, knocked onto its side, empty and unnecessary.

In his state of heightened awareness, he was easily able to locate the logging road and follow it to the car, where Bob was sprawled passed out in the passenger seat. But as soon as Tucker reached the car, he was hit with the enormity of what he had done. The edges of his euphoria began to fray into anxiety.

Tucker pulled up to the Flying J, helped Bob to his room and went to the bar for some towels and the first aid kit. He took off his jeans, washed away the blood on his thigh and poured peroxide into the wound. He knew he should go to the emergency room and have it stitched up, but he also knew the wound would be recognized for what it was and the hospital would be required to report a bear attack. So he made do with the butterfly bandages and gauze from the first aid kit. He put on a clean pair of jeans he kept behind the bar in case of spills or vomiting drunks and threw the old ones in the dumpster behind the Flying J.

By the time he drove through the tunnel at the Buffalo Bill Reservoir near his home, he was trying to frame what he would say to Jen. She would undoubtedly be waiting up for him, worried and angry. How he would love to be able to tell her the truth. But Jen wouldn't understand any more than BobFromAustralia, and she would ruin the experience for him. Worse, she would call his fucking doctor and then the doctor would have him committed and then he would be the one in a cage. Or maybe he would be behind prison bars, and then who would be there to release him? Certainly not Jen! But Tucker remembered a time when Jen would have been in cahoots with him, a time when she was turned on by his fast driving and risk-taking, when she matched his dark humor barb for barb and always had his back when things got out of hand. But that was when she still acted like his wife and not his keeper.

And yet, he wondered, *what if the old Jen's still in there somewhere? What if I went in tonight and told her I've been in the Park letting bears out of traps and she got it and thought it was cool?*

By the time Tucker turned into the driveway, he had managed to convince himself that Jen would be thrilled.

Jen

Tucker didn't call. She had tried calling him but his cell went directly to voice mail. It was either turned off or the battery was dead. No one answered at the bar. She thought about driving to the Flying J, but she knew it would be closed and locked up tight. Besides, this wasn't her first rodeo. Tucker had come home late plenty of times before, always with an explanation and an apology, making her feel foolish for blowing everything all out of proportion.

Jen paced the living room, her eyes trained on the spot in the darkness where the driveway would show itself when he turned onto the property. For the thousandth time, she pressed the button on her Indiglow watch. Four a.m. She repeated her circuit again and again, alternately praying for his safety and cursing him for being an inconsiderate asshole. She moved from the big picture window at the front of the house to the back door in the kitchen, to the window in the family room and back to the picture window.

Finally she heard his car and watched as the mica in the gravel driveway sparkled in his headlights. She tracked the beam up the drive and into the picture window, watched as it wobbled up the wall beside her and disappeared along with the sound of the engine. And then she allowed herself to breathe. *Thank God he's okay.*

In the time it took Tucker to get from his car to the front door, the relief she felt was buried by rage. A rage akin to a herd of bison stampeding through her head, kicking up a blinding dust that hid the Cliff, the place in her mind where she would have to either jump into a bottomless canyon or turn around and fight.

Tucker strode through the door grinning, as if he expected to be met by a big brass band. *Still handsome*, she thought in spite of herself as she looked at him, really looked at him for the first time in quite a while. His blond hair was a little longer than it used to be. It curled onto the collar of his light flannel shirt. He was wearing what Jen thought of as his Wyoming uniform – pearl snapped western shirt, jeans, oversized belt buckle, boots and cowboy hat. It should have looked ridiculous but he wore it easily. His eyes were glazed from too many drugs or not enough sleep and dilated by god knows how much Ritalin Still, they were a startling blue ocean and there was an undeniable gleam in them. He turned towards Jen as he took off his hat. "Hey Babe, I'm glad you're still up. I've had one hell of a night."

"Yeah, so have I. I've been worried sick about you. Where the hell have you been? Why didn't you at least return my call?"

"Aw, Jen," he said, patting his pockets, "I don't even know where my phone is. Anyway, don't be like that. I want to tell you a secret." He walked over to Jen and put an arm around her shoulder trying to pull her into a hug. She pushed him away, nearly gagging at the smell of stale cigarette smoke and beer.

"Did you get my message before you lost your phone?" Jen asked.

"Yeah, I got your message as I was leaving the sanctuary and I was gonna call you as soon as things got quiet at the bar but they never did. But listen to this. You're not gonna believe it." Again he reached out to her and again she slid out of his arms.

"Damn it, Jen, this is important. Can't you just get over the damned phone call long enough to listen to me?"

She knew Tucker well enough to know that he had a whopper of a story to tell, and the part of her that was still able to be charmed by Tucker-the-bad-boy was tempted to engage. But she couldn't afford to give up being mad, not tonight when his behavior had given her just the justification she needed to get on that plane tomorrow.

"You know what, Tucker?" Jen said, "I needed to talk to you about something important too, but as usual it's all Tucker all the time. You're stoned out of your mind and I'm exhausted. I'm getting a migraine and I just can't do this tonight."

"Wait," Tucker said. "Stay up for just a while. I really need to tell you something. And I want to hear what you have to tell me. Have you taken anything for your headache?"

"No, I'm on my way to get it now."

She swallowed her Zomig and was suddenly afraid of what he was going to say. She sensed that it would bring the Cliff too close and she wanted, needed to step back.

"Whatever you have to tell me can wait until tomorrow."

Tucker just crumbled then, along with his fantasy of how Jen would respond. He slid down the wall and sat with his arms wrapped around his knees. Staring straight ahead, he said, "Well, I wish you had been there, babe. It was fucking awesome."

Without responding, Jen made her way down the hall to the bedroom, wanting nothing more than oblivion. But there was something so wistful in Tucker's voice that the oblivion she sought was chased away by a montage of memories of the Tucker she'd fallen so hopelessly in love with. There he was all tanned and gorgeous, laughing, unable to get out of the ocean because the family on the beach would see his hard-on. There he was in his grey suit and perfectly starched white button-down, accepting yet another award for best ad campaign and telling the audience that he could never have done it without his Jen. And there they were in camo, lying under leaves together, trying to be perfectly still, both of them dissolving into giggles every time he tried to call a turkey. The silly, inflatable flamingo that he sent her from Florida so she could feel like she was there with him. The night she picked him up at the airport wearing nothing but lacy underwear, a trench coat and high heels. The postcard that he sent her from Bora-Bora saying *This is the most beautiful place on earth except anywhere that I get to be with you.*

She got up then and retrieved the packet of love letters that she kept in the hat box in the top of her closet. She re-read them as she had done so many times before, trying to remember, trying to believe in a magical bridge that could take them from now back to then. But the sad truth had become so clear to her during her endless night of pacing. She couldn't stop loving Tucker. But she couldn't save him either. All that was left was for her to decide whether she was going down with him.

She took the flattened flamingo out of the bottom of the box and blew it up. When sleep finally found her, tears were drying on her cheeks. Her right arm cuddled the flamingo close to her breast and her left hand was under her pillow, clutching the ticket.

Tucker

Tucker woke in the foyer where he'd curled up the night before. The sunlight poured through the glass of the front door, warming his body but dissipating when it reached the wall surrounding his heart, a heart that was now filled with dread. He had really loaded up on the Seroquel last night and he couldn't quite bring the morning into focus. His tongue stuck to the roof of his mouth and his bladder threatened to burst. As he made his way to the bathroom, he realized that he was already late to meet Marshall at the ranch. They were supposed to work with the wild mustangs that were brought down the mountain yesterday.

I need to call and tell him something, he thought to himself. *This is the third time this month I haven't shown up. He's gonna get disgusted with me and hire someone else.* Tucker ran his hand through his curly blonde hair, trying to smooth and straighten it as he tried to smooth and straighten his thoughts. He needed to appease Marshall because they needed the money he earned at the sanctuary. But more than that, he needed to play a part in rescuing those wild and fearful horses whose acceptance of him validated whatever was still competent and trustworthy in him.

Tucker's "I *can* get better" thoughts raced through his mind, while the healthy side of him tried to wrest control from the unbalanced, irresponsible side. *I wish I could just tell Marshall that this fucking bipolar disorder is kicking my ass and I'm scared it's gonna get worse. It takes every ounce of courage I have just to get out of bed—every ounce of courage and a suitcase full of medicine. Sometimes the medicine evens me out, but it fucks with me, too. It's just as likely to make me feel like a zombie or a superhero. But how do you explain that to somebody?*

Tucker splashed cold water on his face, knowing he wouldn't tell Marshall the truth, knowing there was no way he would understand. *It's Spin the Bottle every morning. Spin the bottle and see which pills fall out first. That's all the fucking doctors do. They're a bunch of modern-day wizards seeking the formula for mental-health gold.*

Tucker added an extra Ritalin to the Sat AM slot in the pill-keeper, emptied the rainbow of pills into his hand and swallowed them dry. He thought of the other pills, the ones that Jen didn't know about, the ones he had saved over time and hidden in the safe after he'd let her convince him to get rid of the guns. She just couldn't see that he *had* to have a way out if it got to be too much to bear.

Tucker sighed, held onto the edge of the sink, closed his eyes and rested his head against the mirror. *You're in Wyoming now, boy, and in Wyoming you just have to cowboy up.*

He walked into the kitchen on autopilot, unaware of the late summer sun reflecting off the crystals in the open window or the smell of sage that came in with the breeze. He poured his coffee and carried it to his recliner, turning on the television as he sat down to wait for the pills and the caffeine to kick in.

He clicked through the networks and settled on the local morning show. When he heard the anchor say "Stay tuned for a terrifying version of Three Little Bears from our reporter at the East Entrance of Yellowstone Park," the insanity of the night before came crashing into his consciousness. *Oh shit.*

Marshall was the least of his problems.

Jen

Jen woke slowly and peeled the plastic flamingo off her cheek where it had migrated during the night. She looked around and saw the letters strewn across the bed; she reached under the pillow and clutched the ticket.

There had been many "mornings after" for Jen, the days she woke up, remembered the current mess in her life, felt the soul-sickness of stark reality and quickly found some way to rationalize it away.

She had written the story of Jen and Tucker on her heart and needed it to be true on such a visceral level that she became blind to any evidence to the contrary. At first it was just a matter of offering explanations she believed were true. If Tucker didn't show up for a dinner party it was because he was exhausted. If he showed up and sat in a chair and pouted all evening, it was because she had upset him before they'd left home. If he snapped at her in front of their friends it was because he hadn't been sleeping well and was understandably irritable.

Over time the explanations became excuses and the excuses became lies. She no longer believed what she said and neither did the people she was saying it to. The messes caused by Tucker's spotty social skills were soon eclipsed by bigger messes like the inability to hold a job and a parade of failed businesses. Eventually the messes became horrors, resulting in gambling debt, arrests, mountains of medical bills for the various broken bones that accompany increasingly risky behaviors, creepy mental hospitals, bankruptcy and a quagmire of disability applications and attorneys. As the horrors grew, Jen's grand love story shrank until all that was left was a sense of duty.

As Tucker descended further and further into the merciless realm of treatment-resistant bipolar disorder, Jen was pulled into a sucking sinkhole of responsibility. She recited her marriage vows to herself relentlessly: *for richer or poorer, for better or worse, in sickness and in health, till death do us part. In sickness and in health, not physical sickness, just sickness. No exemption for mental illness.*

It was such a gradual disintegration so gradually that Jen couldn't say when she had stopped living her life and become Tucker's emotional Siamese twin, joined at their dysfunction. But this morning, lying in bed surrounded by

Tucker's love letters, she knew that she still wasn't ready to face the painful and risky surgery that would be required to sever the connection.

She found herself at the precipice of the Cliff and once again she backed away. Knowing that she was deluding herself even as she thought it, she told herself that they could find a way to make their marriage work. *I'll get up and listen to whatever it is that Tucker was so excited about last night and I'll be supportive and I'll be enthusiastic and maybe there's a good reason that he was so late and he was trying to explain it and I was just being a bitch and, and, and.*

Jen gathered the letters and tied them together with the ribbon from the first gift Tucker had ever given her. She got out of bed, slid open the closet door and replaced the letters in the hatbox, grabbed her robe and went off to find Tucker. She could hear the shower running and thought maybe it would start things off on a happy note if she jumped in with him.

Smiling, she took off her robe and nightshirt and slid open the door to the shower. All her playful intentions washed down the drain along with the blood seeping between the butterfly bandages holding together a ten-inch slice in Tucker's thigh.

"What the hell, Tucker? What happened to you?" Jen immediately reverted to protector mode.

"It's nothing. I had to break up a fight last night and got this for my efforts," he lied, pointing to his injury.

"Did you call the Sheriff's office?"

"Nah, they don't like it at the lodge when we call the law. Looks bad for the place. I just gave them both a cup of strong coffee and sent them back to their rooms."

"Well, why were you so late then? Did you go to the emergency room? I'm surprised they didn't sew that up. It looks pretty deep."

I didn't go to the hospital. We have a first aid kit there and I just cleaned it up real good and stuck these bandages on it. It'll be fine."

"Tucker, it's not fine. It's red and swollen and you need to have it looked at. Come on. Get dressed and I'll drive you to the hospital."

"I'm not going to the fucking hospital." Tucker was agitated now.

Jen was used to this dance. They did it whenever Tucker needed medical attention. *Ever since we moved to Wyoming he's had to be the "cowboyest" cowboy of them all. What a crock of shit.*

"I'm not playing Tucker. Either you get dressed right now and let me take you to the hospital or I'm calling an ambulance. You know I will. You don't need to let yourself get gangrene to prove how tough you are."

Tucker knew she would do it. He was Mama Bear now, caged and angry, and he attacked.

"Goddamn you for the stubborn bitch you are. You can never just back down, can you? Well you're gonna have to back down this time unless you want me to go to prison. Okay?"

Jen felt her toes grasp the edge of the Cliff. "What are you talking about?"

"I didn't get this cut at the bar. I got slashed by a grizzly bear. One of the guys at the bar talked me into going with him to the park and letting a bear and her cubs out of a trap."

"What the fuck, Tucker? You're telling me that you trespassed on Park property and somehow got close enough to bears to pry open steel traps and release their paws? How are you even strong enough to do that?" Jen's voice rose as confusion and hysteria closed in. "Jesus, even if you managed to get away from the bears, those traps could snap your arm in two!"

"Calm down, Jen," said Tucker, grabbing her upper arms with his wet hands. "It wasn't that kind of trap. They were like cages."

"Were they hurt?" asked Jen, trying to find some kind of logic in what he had done.

"No, but Jen, you should have seen that Mama bear. Dammit, that's what I was trying to tell you last night. She was me. I had to let her out."

"What do you mean, she was you? That doesn't make sense, Tucker."

Tucker dropped his arms abruptly, causing her to stumble backwards. "No, it wouldn't make any sense to you. You don't have a fucking clue what it feels like to be me. She was locked up in a cage because somebody like you decided she was dangerous when all she was doing was trying to live in her own damned habitat and take care of her cubs. But she didn't fit in with the plan of turning the park into a fucking money machine by letting the tourists take over so she got put in a cage and she was terrified. She hadn't done anything wrong, don't you get that?"

Tucker's rant was a desert fire burning away what was left of Jen's delusions. She knew it would be pointless to argue with him. He had an unfailing talent for turning the bull's eye on her, and once he started down that path there was no turning him around.

"No, I guess I don't get it Tucker," she said. "You can do what you want about your leg but it looks bad to me." With that, Jen stepped out of the shower and walked toward the bathroom door.

"So now you're just gonna shut down? Just gonna turn on your heel and walk away like you always do?" Tucker taunted. He smelled blood and was going for the kill.

"Yes. That's exactly what I'm going to do."

"Fine," said Tucker. "Get on your high horse and think about what a crazy fucker I am and how superior that makes you. But remember that while you're thinking that I would never walk away from you."

Jen continued out the door, fighting back tears as her mind glommed onto the millions of examples of the ways Tucker had deserted her. And he deserted her again just as quickly as he could get dressed and storm out of the house.

In a daze, Jen collected the items she had listed months ago, knowing that this day was waiting for her. She went to the gun safe and removed her birth certificate, passport and the credit card and cash she had hidden in one of the metal ammo cases. The guns had been removed from the house the last time Tucker threatened suicide, so she'd felt pretty confident hiding it there.

She transferred the cash and card into her wallet and threw it into her carry-on along with her phone, her ticket, a couple of books and the photograph of her mom and dad.

She brought the larger suitcase up from the basement and packed it with as much as she could fit from her closet and chest of drawers.

She sat at her computer and typed a note to Tucker:

Dearest Tucker,

I expect that I know more about what you were feeling when you looked at that bear last night than you would guess. I too have been trapped, locked behind the iron bars of my love for you, my compassion for your suffering, my wedding vows and my fear of what kind of future both of us would face if I were to leave.

So imagine my surprise to realize that the only thing keeping me behind the bars was my own stubborn unwillingness to let myself out. You and I aren't like that bear, Tucker. We get to decide whether or not we want to stay locked up. I've decided to break free of the story of Jen and Tucker that I wrote so long ago, to stop trying to superimpose my fantasy of what I thought we were supposed to be onto the vastly different reality of what we are.

What we are is broken. We hurt each other. We meet on Main Street at high noon nearly every day and aim for each other's hearts. We've both used your bipolar disorder as an excuse for everything that's wrong with us, and it's been very convenient in an incredibly sick way. It lets you off the hook for everything you say and do and it lets me live among the Saints and Martyrs.

But we both know the lie in that. Your illness doesn't give you a pass for bad behavior. And my saintly crown covers a head filled with ugly, angry thoughts. I don't like being that person and I can't seem to be anyone else with you.

Simply put, I can't do this anymore. I won't do this anymore. We both deserve better.

I do love you.

Always,
Jen

P.S: The Jeep is in the long-term parking lot at the Billings airport. The extra key is in the junk drawer.

Jen took the note from the printer, put it in an envelope and tucked it under the edge of the coffee-maker where Tucker would be sure to see it when he came home. She took one last look around, slung her carry-on over her shoulder, released the handle of the wheeled suitcase and rolled it behind her. She walked out the front door, threw her suitcase in the back of the Jeep and headed to the airport. She was at the gate waiting to board when her eye was drawn to a yellow banner that flashed bold type across the bottom of the television monitor: *Breaking News - Tourist family mauled in Yellowstone. Details to follow.* Jen felt the blood drain from her face and form an icy pool in the pit of her stomach. She stared at the monitor and listened to the perky news anchor report the details of her worst nightmare.

KIMBERLY CRUM, MFA, MSW, is the recipient of multiple awards from the Society for Professional Journalists (Metro Louisville chapter) for her magazine profiles and essays. Her work is featured in *New Southerner*, and she has written and performed radio commentary for Louisville's NPR affiliate, WFPL. She teaches undergraduate literature and writing courses at Spalding University and is the sole proprietor of Shape & Flow Writing Services, a writing workshop business.

SLOUCHING TOWARD SELF-ACTUALIZATION: A SEGMENTED ESSAY

"Life comes before literature, as the material always comes before the work. The hills are full of marble before the world blooms with statues."
~ Phillips Brooks, *Literature and Life*

I.

The professor spoke with authority to a room of graduate social work students. We bowed our heads toward spiral notebooks and scrawled notes about Maslow's Hierarchy.

"What a man *can* be, he *must* be," wrote Abraham Maslow. The psychologist believed each of us is able to be "everything that one is capable of becoming." In order to self-actualize, one simply needs to climb from the bottom rung of food-shelter-sex to safety, to love and belonging, to esteem-by-family-and-community. Upon traversing all these, the existential traveler may ascend to self-actualization.

I raised my hand. "Excuse me, sir," I said. "Do you *really* think self-actualization is possible? I mean, when you think about it, only a handful of people have made it that far—Jesus, of course, and Gandhi, and Martin Luther King, and Abraham Lincoln. . . . I mean, do you really expect us to self-actualize our clients, when what they need most is food, safe shelter, a support system and sanity?"

The professor answered my question the only way one should answer a rhetorical question—with silence. Likely, he thought about the psychology of the young woman who had questioned the logic of his claim: "This one is conflicted, emotionally constricted, has unresolved anger issues."

In the intervening years between graduate school and the present, I have thought many times about the professor's claim that we should all aspire to self-actualization. I have walked the miles between "coming of age" and "coming of aging." I have donned several identities: social worker, mother, writer—often, all three at once. I have been unable to assemble the puzzle of my full identity. Isn't it necessary for me to decide *who I am* in order to become *more* of what I am?

Self-actualization is like the Appalachian Trail—many start, but few finish. And there are so many hardships along the way—food shortages, sore feet, loneliness and bears. Many ascend to the trailhead, but few will make it to Maine.

II.

Make a difference, lift the poor from deprivation, give voices to the voiceless, hear real stories stranger than fiction. The latter is the less lofty goal of social work, but it is the truest. People's lives are dramatic, shadowy, strange and triumphant.

A distraught husband shot his wife, my client, and buried her by the reservoir, then turned himself in to the police. Their orphan wandered and wondered.

A single mom's boyfriend disciplined her two-year-old daughter by holding the child in a scalding bathtub. The third-degree burns formed a belt-line across her waist—a recognizable pattern of abuse. Social Services removed the child from her home; the abuser roamed freely. The single mother asked, "Who is punished here?" All I could do was listen.

A man suffering schizophrenia poured gasoline over his head and lit a match. The devil made him do it. Antipsychotic medicines silenced the devil, but the delusions spoke loudly still. He believed the television news was about him. "Don't you see?" he insisted. "They are talking about me!" All I could do was listen.

A man came to the emergency room; he wore a utility belt. "I am Batman," he said. "The garbage men are following me. The Angel Gabriel warned me."

"Does the Angel Gabriel talk to you often?" I asked.

"Oh yes!" he replied, expansively. Batman lives in a world of angels, clandestine plots and superhuman powers —sleeping by night and dreaming by day.

What might I do for people whose intractable misfortunes seem impossible to survive? How might I understand the genuine gratitude of a family whose home was destroyed by fire? "Don't worry about us," the mother said to me, "We'll be fine. We are alive."

All I can do is listen. The world is backwards. The teacher learns from the student: "Don't just do something. Stand there."

III.

I celebrated my first pregnancy for several weeks.

"You either have twins or a cyst," the doctor said. The ultrasound showed a healthy ten-week fetus as well as a tumor on my ovary, as big as a navel orange.

"We will wait for surgery until the genitalia form, at thirteen weeks gestation," the doctor said.

I imagined a little hermaphrodite child or no child at all. After leaving the ultrasound, I walked down the long corridor of University Hospital, sobbing hot tears that seemed not to come from my eyes, but my chest.

The operating room might as well have been Dodger Stadium. The bright lights glared and the crowd assembled —several nurses, one obstetrician, a surgeon, two anesthesiologists, and one pathologist who made a cameo appearance carrying something resembling a Tupperware lunch bucket.

Would the heroic surgeon be able to remove the invader without taking the ovary? Would the villainous cyst be benign or malignant? Would the fetus tolerate the procedure? Would the patient?

"You can't have general anesthetic," the surgeon explained. "You are pregnant." I would have a spinal block, which means I would be awake for the procedure.

"You can't have Valium for the anxiety," the surgeon explained. "You are pregnant."

"You'll feel pressure, but you should not feel pain," the surgeon explained. "Tell me if you feel pain."

"The spinal block might make it hard to breathe," the anesthesiologist said. "Tell me if you're having trouble breathing; I might need to intubate you," he said. I cringed at the thought of the plastic tubing they would insert down my trachea. I promised to breathe.

As the surgeon sliced my abdomen, the anesthesiologist narrated the story of his migration from Beirut, to a residency in Cairo, to this University of Iowa Hospital operating room, where my American lungs relied on his Lebanese expertise.

A green curtain hung between the surgeons and my upper torso. "Is the curtain there so I don't have to watch?" I asked.

Dr. Beirut laughed. And said, "No, the draping is the sterile field. It protects you from infection." Just then, I felt what the surgeon had referred to as "pressure."

Hands pushed against my insides, searching with diligent fingers. I was an empty shell, stuffed and stretched. Like a polyfill toy on a child's bed.

"Breathe slowly," the anesthesiologist warned. He spoke fluent English accented by hyper-enunciated consonants and a foreign lyricism that would have been charming, if I had not thought I was dying.

"Okay," he said in a hushed voice, "Looks like they've got it." His interpretation of the action of my surgery resembled the whispered play-by-play of televised golf tournaments that I often watched with my parents. *And, here comes Nicklaus now, approaching the eighteenth green!*

"It's out!" he announced.

And Nicklaus makes the putt!

"Wow! I haven't seen one this big since I left Cairo." He drew a circle in the air with his hands to demonstrate the size of my amazing neoplasm. "It's as big as a grapefruit! Do you want to see it?"

"Absolutely not."

The pathologist loaded his neon-red lunch bucket to transport the specimen to his laboratory.

"It looks benign," the surgeon said as he embroidered and stapled my abdomen. "Your baby will probably be fine."

"We'll be able to give you a narcotic for the pain, even though you are pregnant," he said. Through the stupor created by exhaustion and morphine, I heard the recovery room nurse talking to the floor nurse. "This one's got a lot of spunk," she said.

I muttered, "I am becoming Real."

IV.

Tracy was a tall blonde woman of pure Norwegian ancestry, a physical therapist on a Burn Center where I was a social worker. We shared a youthful energy for life, as well as daily acquaintance with pain and death in a place where random accidents were the rule. Houses burned. Grain elevators exploded. Chemicals leaked. Scalding water and grease splattered and splashed. Electricity zapped. Victims asked "Why me?" and "What now?" We had no answers to "Why me?" but we became experts on "What now?"

As a physical therapist and a friend, Tracy was willful, bossy and fiercely loyal. You could imagine her in a Viking helmet, standing at the helm of a ship, her flaxen hair blowing about as she issued orders to her crew. Scandinavian stoicism helped her conduct the rigors of motion on reluctant patients whose tender scars contracted like brittle rubber bands across joints, on knees and elbows, shoulders and neck.

"Straighten your arm as far as you can."

"But, it hurts," the patient would object.

"No pain, no gain."

"How can you be so mean?"

"It is not my job to be popular."

Tracy kept a punching bag in her office; it was a multi-purpose stress-reliever. You could punch it or hug it. She bent spoons to relieve the gathering tension that comes from intentionally causing pain. She endured. Among her friends and colleagues Tracy often quipped, "Life's a bitch and then you die."

And then she did.

Within months of the Inflammatory Breast Cancer diagnosis, Tracy lost her hair and was too weak to work. One day while I visited her, she opened a thin hardback book and read out loud her favorite passage from *The Velveteen Rabbit* by Margery Williams. The wise old Skin Horse tells the Velveteen Rabbit how toys become real:

> *Generally, by the time you are Real, most of your hair has been loved off, and your eyes drop out and you get loose in the joints and very shabby. But these things don't matter at all, because once you are Real you can't be ugly, except to people who don't understand.*

Tracy and our burn patients taught me about Real, which means spending less time asking "Why me?" than on contemplating "What now?"

V.

My daughters do not believe in the concept of my youth. They cannot imagine their mother in a headscarf, hoop earrings, overalls and earth shoes. I do not tell them how I danced to the rhythms of live bands, and performed the funky chicken to the cheers of my more inhibited friends. "Yes," I might say, "I asked the same existential questions you seem to be asking. "'Why am I here? What is my destiny?'"

In the 1970's, I found answers in T*he Prophet* by Kahlil Gibran. His poem, "On Children," reflected my parents' shortcomings with these immortal words: "You may give them your love but not your thoughts. For they have their own thoughts." Gibran wrote, "You may strive to be like them, but seek not to make them like you . . . You are the bows from which your children as living arrows are sent forth."

Twenty-five years later, my yellowed copy of *The Prophet* fell from a bookshelf, hitting me in the head. I was no longer in the market for the meaning of life. Instead, I was reading a book titled, *How to Talk So Kids Listen & Listen So Kids Will Talk*. I had become the archer from which my "children as living arrows are sent forth." It was not so easy to be a stable bow "full of gladness" as my arrows hit targets at which I had not aimed.

* * *

My vacuum cleaner choked on a foreign object in the grotto beneath my teenage daughter's mattress. There, I found used tissues, crumpled homework, loose change, dirty socks and the belt Susanna had insisted was lost forever. I also discovered a book wrapped in brown paper. Its pages were dog-eared and its binding was broken. Was this the 21st century equivalent of *The Prophet*? Still kneeling on the floor, I opened the book to a chapter titled "Spells and Incantations," and moved quickly to "What the Wiccan believes" and "Our Mother, the Goddess."

Holding the guide to Wicca in my hands, I paced, motioned the sign of the cross and said aloud, "Holy

Mother of Christ Almighty, my daughter is a witch. Help me out here!"

I waited for a sign. No sign came, but a moment of clarity did. I had been praying to a Holy Trinity. I had directly addressed a Mother Goddess. Could I genuinely condemn Wicca?

"But Mom, it's not my book! Sarah gave it to me, and I don't really believe in that stuff . . . not really." This conditional apology she followed with a rebuttal. "Besides, what do you know about it?"

"Why exactly, would I want to know *anything* about it?" I asked. Nevertheless, I agreed to learn more about what I defined as "witchcraft." I logged on to www.wiccan.com.

I agreed with part of my daughter's defense of Wicca—its guiding philosophy is "Do no wrong," and "Yes, Catholicism does contain ritual ceremonies and incantations," and "Yes, if you must assign a gender to God, it is fine to see Her as female," and, "Okay, I'll agree that Wicca is not inherently evil."

I shuddered at the words I had spoken.

VI.

My daughter Liz said, "Mom. Why is your skin blotchy? Why do the veins on your hands stick out so far?" I laughed and said, "I am becoming Real." She looked at me blankly, not having been patient enough to sit through the story of the *Velveteen Rabbit*.

I am a cliché of aging. I have creaky knees, age spots, laugh lines and "natural highlights" in my dark brown hair. The skin of my upper arms waves when I do. None of this bothers me. What troubles me is the acceleration of time—the growing up and the letting go. My parents are now spirit people. My daughters are flesh and spirit, traversing the two worlds where child and woman meet. They are the new toys in the house—with fresh skin stretched taut over curvy frames. Their eyes sparkle with possibility.

Dr. C is a psychologist and my spiritual director. He helps me with the rigors of becoming Real. He is my gray-haired, bearded guru with a ponytail who serves herbal tea then waits for me to speak. He is very comfortable with silence—what psychotherapists call the "pregnant pause." One could easily meditate or do a ritual dance in Dr. C's office, where Native American artifacts decorate the walls and dim lighting casts soothing shadows.

I know it hurts, but stretch. No pain, no gain.

"We all have shadow selves," he says. Dr. C is a Jungian, which means he believes in the soul, religion, dreams and the unconscious self. He does not wish to fix me; I am who I am. He is a seeker, not a soothsayer. He is my Skin Horse.

I speak about my recent acquaintance with grief, an experience hard to describe but you know it when you feel it. I tell him how I sob spontaneous hot tears at images, smells and sounds that remind me of my parents—the sight of fall leaves, the sound of Nat King Cole, the hush of televised golf tournaments, and the memory of vodka martinis: "very dry, no fruit."

Dr. C and I talk about the value of suffering, why bad things happen, and how we can make sense of the unexpected. He says everyone has a destiny. Fate is what happens. How you react to random life events determines your destiny.

"I'm not in any real rush to get to my destiny," I joke. I am whistling in the dark. *Is there a monster under my bed? Something scary just around the corner? Do I really want to know my shadow self?*

When I am silent, Dr. Cunningham waits. There is no rush. The words will come. He knows what Tracy and the Skin Horse knew: "[Real] doesn't happen all at once. You become. It takes a long time."

The social worker tries to repair broken lives. The mother guides and protects the child. The writer attempts to capture life on paper. Failing to receive the blessing of the muse, the writer's words falter. The social worker cannot reverse the hurt. Children are living arrows flying in a direction they determine. Fate we do not choose.

At the door of Dr. C's office hangs a plaque: "Vocatus atque non vocatus, Deus adent." Translated from the Latin this means "Beckoned or not beckoned, god(s) will be present."

VII.

There is solace for the traveler on the self-actualization trail. Though few of us will complete the hike, there is consolation for the journeyer. Maslow believed that it is possible for everyone to have "peak experiences," moments of clarity, awe and self-awareness, when we suddenly understand why we exist.

My peak moments are not confined to visions of beauty, when the sun sets scarlet over the tops of trees or a sudden rain shower creates a rainbow at midday. Peak moments occur when my feet are sore from pounding the rocky path and I slouch into territory I do not recognize—when I am lost and don't know which way to turn, when I am weary and cannot walk another step.

But I do.

FREDERICK POLLACK is author of two book-length narrative poems, *The Adventure* and *Happiness*, both published by Story Line Press. His work appears in *Hudson Review, Salmagundi, Poetry Salzburg Review, Die Gazette* (Munich), *The Fish Anthology* (Ireland), *Representations, Magma* (UK), *Bateau, Chiron Review, Big Bridge, Hamilton Stone Review, Diagram, BlazeVox, The New Hampshire Review, Mudlark, Occupoetry, Faircloth Review, Camel Saloon, Kalkion, Gap Toothed Madness* and others. Frederick is an adjunct professor of creative writing at George Washington University.

CARES OF A DRAGON

To the East he is luck and strength, even
justice – the hero you know
rides in for you at last. To the West,
he's the flying nag of some outmoded evil.
It's this that makes him writhe and snap:
he'd like to mean one thing.

To test his flame against skyscrapers
and drones, as once against castles and arrows—
to what end? A B-movie gurgle;
not even a tear from the hero's girlfriend.
But when he imagines vast, righteous
uprisings, he hears firecrackers
and banging cans, and feels crowds,
paid by the hour, under his tassels.

Sometimes the nymphs of polluted
or vanished rivers come to weep
on his scales; he strokes their cheeks with clumsy claws.
And sometimes grander gods, resigned, even
happy to be rentiers
of abstraction, descend for tea.
For in the boring realm of archetypes,
ideas have nothing to do
but visit. They know enough to leave
when he asks, *"Shall I warm your cup?"*

Immortal spirits should be spared
ambivalence, the dragon rages.

Or is it secretly the godlike state? –
In any case his one remaining
stable role is to brood,
curl upon curl, on his hoard.
Which is, he would protest, however,
himself, not gold. Only lesser
beings would imagine being this way for money.

THE REVOLT OF THE ANGELS

The sensitive one hopes
this inland sea dried
slowly enough for people simply
to leave. But coolly as ever,
his companion points
to the remains of a hand
emerging from rubble. Waits,
disdainful yet as always
impassive, as the sensitive one
kneels, bows his head,

and weeps. Same histrionics
as at the broken reactor,
and the functioning torture center
a thousand miles east.
There he reached out
in anguish towards the victims, but
accomplished no more
than in former days. The insensitive one
speaks now; outlines
the politics and religions

of the region. The sensitive one
pays no attention;
knows that all data,
in the absence of any other
chronicler, are stored
in the arcana of matter –
his friend's dry summaries are merely

cruel. He has soiled
his white robe, kneeling;
it returns to whiteness as he stands.

His friend, currently female,
suggests they exchange
genders if not characters
for the upcoming stretch.
"I'm sorry," smiles the first, "I'll stop
going to pieces."
"It isn't that," she says.
They proceed again across
that landmass and the others,
satisfied with space-time
and the habit of witness.

RENE MULLEN is a copyeditor for a public relations firm in Albuquerque, and volunteers as a Court Appointed Special Advocate and NaNoWriMo Municipal Liaison.

THE DEVIL INSIDE

The Good Book teaches us, well-behaved women act a certain way. I'm one of them women. In my home, I stands tall, quiet. City folk think we just walk about in bare feet, kicking up pig dung and spitting out children. Truth be told, we do our part. They do theirs. That's the way the world works. That's how it's always worked.

Taking some new-fangled dish soap my husband bought from the city, I hope he'll like his supper tonight. I wring my hands out on the same faded burlap towel used since momma did these dishes. Just the way the world works. He tries. I know he does. A chip in one of the bigger saucers sends me back.

That child of mine. What a handful.

Never listens. Does whatever she wants. Something's broken with that one. I tell you. Not how I raised her though. No way. Raised her like a proper girl. Wasn't till she started schooling she came down with a case of the overalls and chopped off hair. Looks like a dang-gum boy.
Through the window I looked out for so many years, I sees the tree she played Tea Time under. Them were better days. She a changed one now. No more Tea Time. No nothing time. Just stays out the house like we got the sickness or something.

For a moment, I think I sees her holding that tea cup all proper like. Always smiling. Always giggling like a woman should.

I giggle, though I try not to.

She should do right though.

She fades away in my mind as something comes over the hill, way back yonder. Ain't nobody run like that in these parts since my pappy died mid-sleep while back. My hands go dry as my heart stops itself dead. Who is it?

Little better in, I see the overalls. I lose sight of her as I roll my eyes. Nobody around, so I can do what I want. Nobody telling me I ain't acting proper. Closer still, I see that dang-gum mark. That Devil's Mark. On her cheek.

She say she got it tussling with a boy. I say she ain't doing it right. But I know better. Wasn't no boy. Was the Devil Himself. Since that mark hopped up on her face, it's been nothing but trouble round here.

That's when she started dressing funny. Talking funny too. Sometimes not at all. When she does, it's Devil words. Two weeks later, momma run off. Left me to care for pappy and my own family. Ain't right. But that's how it works.

Week after that, pappy died. Nobody know why. Least that's what they say. I know different. She does the Devil's work. It's that dang-gum mark. Can't prove nothing. Don't need to. A woman know these things.

"Momma," someone screams.

It's my babe. But her voice ain't one I heard in a Mark's age. I think it's my memories, playing games. The Devil tempting me to things that ain't real. Then I hear again. Same as before.

"Momma," my babe yells.

I rub my eyes with momma's towel, look again. She dressed like the Devil, but she sounding like my babe.

"Oh Babe," I yell out the window that ain't been a window in two years. "What is it, babe?"

"Come quick," she hollers in the innocent voice I know from before. Fear of God is all over her, but I can't help smiling. My babe is back. Then I see the Devil's Mark and I think it's a trick. I can't help it.

"What is it, child?"

"Poppa. It's poppa, momma." She yells from under that crabapple tree. Behind her fear, I see my babe again. Even behind that mark. Dang-gum scar. My heart pushes to my mouth. My Man. Oh my Heaven, my Man is in trouble.

I run out the back door, not ladylike at all.

"What is it, child," I screams. "What's happened to my Man?"

"Poppa," she says as she leans over to catch her breaths. "Poppa fell off the cliff."

She grabs me by the arm, all rough, the way he does. I already scared. All kinds of stories plays out inside me. Him all busted up, laying in the creek bed. His blood all over the forest.

We run. We run so long, my chest feels dry, my breasts are sore. They good for child rearing, not for running. Not for well-raised ladies.

Over the hills, she drags me to the woods. Trees slap my face. I'm used to that sort of dealings.

Another couple hills with branches slapping me. I see the cliff ahead through a break in the growths. My chest's going explode on itself. I know it. But I don't care. My Man's hurt.

He's spread out on the ground like some drunk nights I find him. First I thinks I see him breathing. Then he's not. My Man's not breathing.

***

Sheriff comes to "take names" and makes nice talk with me and my babe. No tears like I thought I would. I gots my babe back. She comes and hugs me. We both looks at my Man. I look down at her. She smiles something funny. Then I knows. A woman always knows.

The Devil's gone. I gots my babe back. That's how it works. I squeezes her. The Devil inside her's gone too.

MARIUS SURLEAC, author of Zeppelin Jack (Herg Benet, 2011) is a Vaslui, Romania-born physicist, poet, and prose writer. He publishes mostly in Romanian journals, and also has poetry appearing in international journals: *Pif Magazine*, *Mad Swirl*, *Poetry Super Highway*, *Atlas Poetica*, and *Boston Poetry Magazine*, *Bare Fiction* (UK), *Dear Sir* (Austria), and *Novo Slovo* (Serbia). He translates Romanian poetry by Marc Vincenz, Valzhyna Mort, and Peycho Kanev. His Romanian translation of "The Propaganda Factory, or Speaking of Trees," by Marc Vincenz, will be published in bilingual form at Adenium publishing house this year.

BIPOLAR

by Christmas everything was settled with the pork
meat immortalized in its own fat in transparent jars
the pieces of wood irregularly cut and broken by axe
moving their tiny fibres right into our noses in a no
perspective riding on snowflakes before reaching stove
dad's in the forest searching for spruce with the cheeks
fighting the crivetz
mum preparing cheese and apple pies and pound cakes
snow crosses above the wooden fence and passers are
closer to the sky every roof whispers the white smoke
and I don't know if we fall up or flakes rise down

we pour hot wine with pepper and cinnamon in clay mugs
with my thoughts distributed all over the rooms and foyer
I think about my other brothers living near Gobi desert
themselves thinking to the other me dressed in a Carpathian
bear & dancing in a very cold trance & dye on my spirit

GAZERS

and so we sat   on the seafront   one thousand elephants
boisterously   sucking   lemonade   with bamboo sticks
dreamingly   licking   one thousand   colored lollipops
            reddish log   suckers making   the waves' delicate touch
oscillating   thick   ears   like springboks hop up the cords
            of our fellows that triggered   us down one thousand
cigars   wasted through shells behind   the dusk
&   blank pages   float down   on our gaze

JON SINDELL's short fiction appears in *Hobart, Word Riot, Zouch, New South, Prick of the Spindle, Switchback, Crack The Spine, Weave* (upcoming), and elsewhere. A human, he earns his bread as a personal humanities tutor. He curates the Rolling Writers reading series in San Francisco for kicks, and practiced law once't.

A MAN FORBID

"Sleep shall neither night nor day
Hang upon his penthouse lid;
He shall live a man forbid…"
~ Weird Sister, *Macbeth*

Soil rich, black, and damp yearned like a woman awaiting the seed. The sleeper's lips trembled as he beheld a single seedling emerging from the dirt, teardrop leaves of luminous green arching out from its crotch, the earth dark and moist as the gigantic wedges of cake in the magazine ads his mother would paste to the fridge like a dream of home life. In these ads the cake was dark, moist, layered with buttercream, and the edge of the fork sliced into the cake the way the dreaming man's hoe had cut into the rain-sodden soil of the vegetable garden just an hour before. The dreamer's mother had made these cakes as a Sunday treat when he was small and there were still four at home, and he'd gorged on them till his stomach ached. Then, in the hot, nasty summer when he was fourteen and there were just the two of them left, she made them all the time, and he shunned them to shun her, and counted out loud each bite that she took, and she'd lower her head to eat in a shamed, petulant way, chewing like a cow masticating; then when she'd finish, he'd skate around the corner and take one toke on a joint and one pull on a beer for every one of her bites.

In the dream she wore the orange-and-yellow flowery thing she called a "muu-muu" because it made her feel as if she were in Hawaii, persisting in spite of Iris's snide, "It's a *dress*, Mama," in spite of her husband calling it a horse blanket, in spite of her son calling it a tent when he was twelve to raise Papa's bitter smile. He worked hard every night to copy that smile in the mirror, and when Papa left for good, he perfected it without effort. In the dream she was thirty or forty, yellow-haired, double-chinned, shapeless in her muu-muu, standing on the bare ground of an ill-defined park, scooping moist black earth with her dish-red hands, reaching out mounds of earth with a smile innocent of the heartaches to come—the smile he remembered from when he was four.

"Do you like it, Mackey? Do you like it again?" He moaned, "I do like it" and reached out, but the guard smashed his baton against the heavy metal key-plate and Mack shot up screaming.

Officer Padik was as big as an offensive lineman, with a round face slitted by eyes that gleamed and thin lips that curled with the pleasure of making Mack scream. Mack sat up at an acute angle to the officer, cradled his face in cracked hands, blinked tears from his eyes. Angered by the lack of eye contact, the guard strummed his baton across the bars the way Mack at fourteen had clattered the wrought-iron fences in "the nice folks' neighborhood" with his bat, awakening weekend sleepers. One silver-haired man growled "Barefoot trash," and Mack slashed his tires the next day and fled into the woods, where his friends raised their beers to anoint "Mack the Knife."

"Sleeping in the daytime?" the guard asked with mock shock. "How the hell you gonna get ahead in life if you sleep in the daytime?" The guard puffed up with his wit, but Mack didn't respond. "I'm talking to you!"

The officer banged the door, and Mack looked up at him through red eyes sunk into sockets as wide and deep as goldfish bowls. The guard probed the prisoner's countenance for any sign of dissent, but there had been no dissent since Mack's first night in jail three years before, when the guard had delivered two expert blows to his shins with his baton as he slept, "expert" inasmuch as they delivered great pain without any telltale fracturing of bone.

"Lemme show you something," said the guard.

Mack stepped gingerly to the bars, and the guard thrust a wallet photograph at his face. "She's beautiful. Isn't she!"

It was the shiny, black, extended-cab pickup that the officer had purchased two months ago.

"That didn't come from sleeping all day." He snorted contemptuously and peered down at Mack . "Got a surprise for you. You're gonna get a new roommate! And you're really gonna like this one, Mack—a new friend to have sleepovers with, a person to tell your secrets to. Hell, Mack, you are such a good friend."

But the roommate wasn't due for several more days, and the delay had the effect that Officer Padik intended. Mack was chronically jumpy from lack of sleep to begin with, and this new anxiety wore his nerves wire-thin. In the mess hall, in the library, in the exercise yard, he jerked his head at fellow prisoners in the suspicion that they knew the nature of the new torment that awaited him and were laughing at him. Only in the vegetable garden did he find any peace. He knelt on the rain-sodden soil and worked it with his trowel, feeling himself the kindly god of the patch of earth shadowed by his body. He had a mellow gardening friend known as Gen'ul G, an enormous reformed dealer from Hunter's Point who likewise sought solace in the soil. Everything the big man knew about gardening he had learned from Mack, who had learned an enormous amount about the cultivation of veggies—and weed—in his youth in the Ozark foothills. G passed behind Mack with a hoe on his shoulder, and when his enormous shadow covered Mack's little kingdom, Mack sprung up into a knife-fighter's crouch with the trowel in his hand.

Gen'ul G laughed: "Mack the Trowel, what a fool."

Mack lay on his back like a vampire in his coffin, arms folded across his chest, neck stiff as rigor mortis. He failed to fall asleep for two hours, then slept, then dreamt that a shadow—black and shapeless as a vampire's cloak, or an oil slick, or a black ectoplasm, or a giant bat ray, or Gen'ul G's shadow—hovered over his head and began to descend to smother him. He shot up again, and slept no more that night.

Officer Padik shoved the new roommate, Anthony, into the cell the next morning. He was thin and thirtyish, with sallow, pock-marked cheeks; soft, dewy eyes sunk deep in black sockets; and hair dyed artificially black.

"You guys are gonna get along like peas in a pod," Padik chortled. "Like Anthony and Cleopatra. Just don't turn your backs on each other."

In a comic burlesque of a kind father closing his sons' bedroom door for the night, Padik blew a soft kiss and stepped away—then whirled like a discus-thrower and crashed his baton against the door. The new guy jumped and shrieked.

Mack judged Anthony to be harmless due to his scrawny build, nervousness that was extreme even for a new guy, and especially his eyes. Mack had known dangerous men on the streets of the Tenderloin and in Golden Gate Park, where he'd made his last camp, and this guy's eyes lacked their menacing glint.

And then the guy started talking in a thin, high voice, treating time as a space to cram full of words:

"Alright, so, um, like, well—and what are you in for? Uh huh, uh huh. Okay, never mind! That was rude to ask, just please don't be angry, oh please, honey, won't you cut me some slack? I mean, imagine how I feel right now. I mean, look: I bet the new meat always chatters like that. Oh, they do? Uh huh, uh huh, see I told you they do, of course they do, sure they do, all like chatter-chat-chat, hey, that's normal, that's my own normally abnormal way anyway, I just roll like that, I chatter like a chipmunk, got to fill my cheeks . . ." a ladylike hand covered a naughty mouth, "let me start over. Okay, I mean. Look. My god. I mean, honestly. And just what the hell else is there to do in a place like this except talk talk talk? A place like this!" he laughed hysterically, "as if there are actually places like this! Well, I suppose we could—I don't know . . . decorate, maybe! I mean, gawd, these white walls are just gorgeous with those cute cracks in the plaster, and that picture of—ooh, that's sort of like—a stock car, right? Wow, I'm rooming with the Duke of Hazzard! That's a joke, don't kill me! Omigod, oh god, I am absolutely gonna die in here!"

He snuffled hysterically, gasped for air like an asthmatic, then stood up straight with his chin raised high in perfect dignity.

"No, honey, I assure you: you most certifiably did NOT get a fruitcake for your cellmate. A cellmate! Omigod, oh-my-sweet-fucking-god, I'm a cellmate in a prison, and I am fucking going to die! Thank you, you're sweet—oh, and you gave me a clean tissue, too! Stop looking at me, I was making a joke!" Sniffling turned to sobbing. "I just wanted to say that you're a fine host, a real country gentleman, and that is no—oh, what's that fucking word—aspersion, that's no aspersion on your country background—my god, like I should talk, I'm from Hicksville Oregon, that's just rednecks with guns. Oh please, god, please, would you please stop looking at me with those cold blue eyes, I don't even know where you're from! And if I did know, I'd love it, I love everyone from wherever they come from, don't you get it? So, where do you come from? Oklahoma? No? Texas? No? Thank gawd it's not Texas. Arkansas? I knew it! Hey, a president came from there, that's nothing to be ashamed of at all. Don't look at me like that! You're killing me," he said between sobs, "I didn't say there's anything wrong with it at all, I said just the opposite in fact, if you'd care to look up the record. Help me, I'm gonna be sick! I need cigarettes! Thank you ... you're a gent." A soft furtive hush: "Hey—do you know how to get some coke in this place? Crack, maybe? What's that shrug mean? No, you can't get it, or no, you don't trust me? Never mind, I agree: we just met; we're not there yet. Sigh. You know, I could get those things out on Polk Street with a snap of my fingers ... I'm not bad looking, though this lighting's from hell. I could ... you know ... do things ... Christ, would you please stop looking at me!"

"I'm listening to you," Mack said.

"Oh yeah?" Through narrowed eyes he peered at Mack. "Then listen to this. I may be a queer, but nobody—and I mean, nobody—fucks with me. The last time a john tried to steal my wallet I stuck him right in the ass with a great big fucking pair of kitchen scissors, so—omigod, sit down!" He scurried back up onto his cot and balled himself small against the wall.

"Please sit down," he sniffled, gasping for breath, "I was kidding, just kidding! God, please let me out of this place!"

Anthony closed his eyes and shivered all over, then squeaked in a constricted little voice that barely made it through his windpipe: "Help me, man. I am gonna get murdered in here."

Mack knit his brow and pondered the circumstances. "No," he said with a sober air. "You're not. You got me, and G—he's got pull with the brothers. We give 'em extra veggies from the garden. It's supposed to go to some restaurant or something, but ... you'll be cool. You won't even have to—."

"Omigod, how I love you! Omigod, think of that—I love crackers in bed!"

Anthony leaned back in alarm. "Omigod, that's a joke! Don't you know me by now?"

Mack sat back down, and Anthony, calming himself with a visible effort, subdued his tone.

"So what did you object to, anyway: the cracker, or the bed? Ah, you smiled! I knew you could smile. See, you just gotta know me, Sugar. Every time I open my big pretty mouth it gets me in trouble—oops, I did it again!" he sung out like Brittany Spears. "Change the subject fast, Ladybird!"

Anthony straightened his back, crossed slender legs and skinny arms, and mimed holding a cigarette like a cocktail party hostess.

"Okay, so new topic. Tell me, Arky: Do you like marbles?"

"What?" Mack smiled in spite of himself.

"Or cheetahs? Or Cheetos? Or— Christ, I don't know. Do you like . . ." Anthony spiraled his fingers in front of himself, as if to pluck conversational fodder like grapes from a vine. "Antelopes? Or artichokes? Or spring rolls, perhaps? There's a Vietnamese place on O'Farrell, and the guy at the counter pretends that he's straight, but we know he's queer as a flamingo taquito; and the spring rolls in there— "

Hours later Anthony was still talking.

"Jesus," said Mack. "You are one wired dude."

"I'm a ... wired sister!" trilled Anthony.

"Yeah, well, Wired Sister, I need some sleep."

Anthony leaned across the space separating the cots. "If I sleep I'll die."

"I'll die if I don't."

In a tremulous hush the new prisoner said, "It's scary in here. Don't you think I could sort of—you know—just, like, creep on over there and get under the covers, snuggle up a little, like a sleepover thing— "

"No."

With stiff-necked dignity the new guy replied, "Then goodnight, Mr.— I don't believe I caught your last name?"

"Betts. Mack B." Mack initiated a firm, traditional American man's handshake, warning Anthony with a hard gaze to respond in kind. "Now go to sleep, man."

Anthony lay flat on his back, eyes open. He continued to talk but reduced the volume of the chatter he directed at the phantoms in the ceiling such that Mack could tune it out like a neighbor's radio.

But Mack couldn't sleep. In the post-midnight stillness the incessant murmurings of his cellmate came into sharp focus like conversation on the other side of a thin flophouse wall, and he could not tune out the endless stream of words.

"Shut up," he barked, but that switched on muffled sobbing, so he grumbled "forget it" and clamped his eyes shut.

He fell asleep hours later, and then he dreamt he was lying in Golden Gate Park in the pup-tent-sized hollow of a gnarled tree that he and Janine had called home for three months. They tore down camp every morning before the park gardeners showed up, and then made camp again at sundown when the civies were gone. In the dream, he and Janine had just shot up, and, as the drug came on, he laid face down on his bedroll, resting his splotched face on the puffed-up sleeve of the jacket he'd scored at Goodwill.

"Hey," Janine said with the feather-soft murmur, ragged at the edge, that signaled her desire and aroused his, and he smiled at her—oh, how she loved the way his smile raised the plunging edges of his mustache and made him look boyish. In the dim twilight, she looked closer to the twenty-eight that she was than the leathery forty the daylight made

her appear, and her dimpled cuteness and mini-Oreo eyes
filled him with wild tenderness. He rolled onto his back and
closed his eyes in anticipation of receiving her body, but a
sudden premonition of evil opened his eyes to the killer
from Psycho standing above him with his arm raised high
—but it wasn't a knife but a huge pair of scissors gleaming
in the darkness, and it wasn't a movie killer. It was
Anthony plunging the scissors down towards his heart.

He rolled over violently before the scissors could land,
arousing Anthony from a superficial doze. "What's
wrong?" Anthony murmured in a soft maternal tone. Mack
stared at him in a catatonic daze, and Anthony insinuated
himself to a standing position and took a first tentative step
across the floor like a tightrope walker three-hundred feet
above ground; when Mack didn't move, he slide-stepped
once more and stood next to his cellmate. Mack looked up
at Anthony: the harsh white light from the naked bulb in the
corridor directly across from the cell illuminated his deep
black death's-head eye-sockets. Anthony lowered himself
with the caution of a bomb squad technician and the
delicacy of a ballerina and wrapped his skeletal arms
around Mack's shoulders. Mack shuddered and threw them
off.
"I understand," said Anthony, raising his chin and then
his whole body with formal dignity. "It'll be alright, baby."
He touched a soothing finger to his lips. "If you need me
just say so. I don't ever sleep, really."
So Mack laid back down and tightened his face in a
grim mask fit to scare away demons. He sang Johnny Cash
and Merle Haggard tunes in his head for an hour and more,

then slept, then dreamed once more. In the dream, he was twelve again, asleep in his bedroom before dawn, and the twelve-year-old sleeper was dreaming too, walking through the nice folks' neighborhood on the way to the good ball yard with its grass infield, raised pitcher's mound, and outfield fences. He was walking in the exact center of the street, inhaling the sweet alyssum that grew along the wrought-iron fences of the nice folks' homes, but he didn't dare turn his face to the blossoms but looked straight ahead, shielding his eyes from the blinding white light that pervaded the air and burned his lungs. On impulse he took off running and kept running until he reached a cool green field that was not the ball field, but was the ball field. His friend John was there, sitting on his bike—why, oh why, had he turned against John? Or was it the reverse? And all of a sudden, it no longer mattered—for John, swathed in golden light, smiled at him, and he dared smile back. But in the outer dream, the dream of a dreamer, his father, in the power company hard hat he wore during Mackey's twelfth summer, shook him hard by the shoulders. "Get up, candy ass. If I can get my ass outta bed at this god-damned hour, you sure as hell can too," and the twelve-year-old dreamer looked up at his father with wide dish-eyes and a wide-opened mouth to speak the words he never had dared— "

"Get up, punks!" Officer Padik banged the baton on the lock plate and strummed the bars. A smile bloomed on his face when the cellmates raised themselves, bleary-eyed, to a sit.

In the library, as they called it, there was a psychology section comprised of two textbooks, neither of which answered Mack's desperate question: How to resume a truncated dream? A middle-aged long-timer named Nemo with some nebulous claim of a connection to Stanford, which was supported by his scholarly appearance—spectral frame, wispy chin, weak blue eyes that beamed out through round wire frames—as if to imply that the man occupied a secret world of knowledge and wisdom to which he'd gladly conduct you, if you were worthy and able (highly doubtful).

Nemo stroked his chin and allowed that, yes, certainly, there must be an answer to this fascinating question, which has challenged thinkers and seekers throughout the ages. "Of course, in ancient Greece, in *The Odyssey*, as you know (he chuckled ironically but not cruelly), reference is made to the lotus eaters, which is not discordant with historical fact. For there is, indeed, evidence that the ancient Greeks, lofty thinkers and dreamers that they were, used opium. *Shhhhh.*" A finger to his lips stifled a chuckle occasioned by the prisoner's mention of one of the multitude of psychotropic drugs for which he had been imprisoned—opium, aka nepenthe, as in, nepenthe, as in, 'quaff this nepenthe, help me forget my lost Lenore'—from "The Raven" of course! Nepenthe induces forgetfulness, and is that not akin to dreaming, shutting out external stimuli, allowing the subconscious mind to roam freely?

"Ahh, we're getting somewhere! A plausible means to reenter dreams! Perpend: For as I say, the ancient Greeks utilized various psychotropic drugs as a means of accessing certain portals of the mind. These portals, as we call them, may allow access to various points in the mind, points of consciousness. And studies suggest—reveal!—that the situs of memory can be geographically mapped in the brain to the hippocampus. ("Not a college for hippopotami," he chuckled). And is a dream, once dreamed, not a memory too? And so, does it not stand to reason that memories themselves can be mapped, accessed, and retrieved from definite sites, s-i-t-e-s?

"Now, if you will permit me a brief digression. Consider that certain mind-expanding substances are somewhat analogous to training wheels on a bike, *id est*, a training device that can ultimately be dispensed with once the desired skill is attained, or if you think of a pianist practicing blindfolded in order to deepen his purely aural awareness of the music—the subtle intonations, reverberations, undertones, harmonics—Gregorian chants come to mind, as do . . ."

Mack slipped away, with Anthony trailing five-feet behind. Not necessarily close enough to invite a beating by other inmates, but close enough for Anthony to enjoy the illusion of safety. Mack laid himself down, determined to return to the bright green ball field and his lost friend, John, and lay for hours in his vampire position, trying various methods to fall aasleep. Merle Haggard couldn't do it. Johnny Cash couldn't do it—and, to his horror, he discovered that he couldn't recall the words to "Long Black Veil," though he'd sung himself to sleep with the song hundreds of times. So he tried to visualize the most soothing image he could think of: the bright green mustard seedlings that were just then emerging in his prison garden plot. But every time he managed to summon a clear image, he was snapped out of his reverie by the terrified mutterings of his cellmate, who was lying flat on his back staring at the ceiling as the harsh white light of the corridor filled the bowls and crevices of his face.

He tried tuning out Anthony but that didn't work, so he tried the opposite, tuning into Anthony's words the way he had strained to hear *America's Most Wanted* or *COPS* in his parents' room after bedtime. That worked for a while, for his mind was drawn away from itself by Anthony's fragmented mumbling about knives in the ass and thieving johns and God! Don't! No!, but he was jolted into full wakefulness by the recollection of his father snapping, "Get to fuckin' sleep in there!" which often preceded the sound of angry rutting.

So he decided to count monster trucks rolling over Civics, but the trucks dissolved into switchblade knives hanging in mid-air dripping blood onto his black garden plot, and then the knives became blood-dripping scissors, and the lack of sleep became the physical pain of the skin of his face flaking off like roast pork sliced from the bone.

He shot upright and realized that the whole thing had been a dream of lying there awake.

Hours later he fell back to sleep and dreamed that he was wearing a golden crown like the one from his fifth birthday party, when his dad had passed through the living room snorting, "We all know who's the real king around here."

But in the dream he was twelve, not five, and he met John again on the grass of the ball field. He hailed him as "King John!" but John charged off into the woods on his bike, so Mackey took off after him on bare feet flying over the wet grass and dove into the woods as if sliding head-first into second base, landing on the bed of soft leaves that Janine laid beneath their bedrolls in their little encampment in the park every night. "Safe," said Janine, but there was mockery on her lips and a reproachful hardness in her small, black eyes, the look she got when she'd been too long without scag, which was always his fault. She could have been a singer. She'd received beer money and twenty bucks cash singing R&B with a band in Stockton last year, and she hadn't even had to put out. And what the hell was she doing with a loser like him?

"C'mon, Janine," he told her, flopping onto his back and flashing the grin that she couldn't resist.

But she threw her chin up in the air and shook her head No! No! No! The terror of being without the drug aroused in her hysterical laughter that melted into weeping.

"C'mon, baby," he said, sitting up and wrapping his arms around her heaving body, softly stroking her musty hair. She seemed to calm down, cocked her head at him in a calculating way, pushed him back by the chest and down onto the bedroll and climbed up onto him—but her eyes looked off to the kayak-sized hollow a few feet from theirs in which a college dropout from Michigan had been sleeping for weeks. Mack saw the look and woke up with cold sweats.

He had one tab of acid. It had cost him four bunches of baby carrots, a prize artichoke, five packs of cigarettes and twelve dollars cash, and he'd saved it for a special occasion. The pseudo-Stanford man had spoken of reentering dreams by psychotropic means; it seemed worth a shot. He swallowed the tab and lay down to wait, but the exhaustion from two-plus sleepless nights overcame him and he lapsed into sleep. Whether he came on to the drug before he dreamt or no, he was back in the park and Janine was atop him. She held a forty-ounce can of malt liquor over her head, extended her tongue below the mouth of the can to catch the last precious drops, and then threw the can onto a pile of empties. She lowered her mouth to his ear and softly whispered "loser," which filled him with swirling anger and desire. She lifted herself up laughing hysterically, shuddered violently, threw her head back. She seemed far above him even before her neck began telescoping upward like Alice's after eating the cake, and when her head was near the canopy of the eucalyptus trees, she gazed down with red dragon eyes at the kid from Michigan sleeping nearby.

Then she was herself again, sexy and cute, and she rocked her hips hard upon him. He tried to pull her down to maneuver her into the bedroll, but she thrust a stop sign in his face, then lowered her mouth to his ear and said in a soft, ragged hush, "He's got scag, man. That stinking slumming rich boy's been holding out on us, and we've fed him for weeks. And you kept him getting rolled by those punks! You know," she said with an expert modulation down to a soft key, "He's been eyeing me, man, when you're not around. You know, he is kinda cute." She flicked his ear with her tongue, breathed warm breath into his ear. "Called you a cracker."

What a sweet voice she had! And how sweet she smelled. Somehow, although homeless, she managed to smell nice. Then she convulsed from the agony of twenty-one hours without smack, seized the neck of his jacket and lifted his head, shook it up and down in rhythm to words barked through ragged tears: "What the hell do you care, man! You never do nothing for me, nothing! And you say you're a man!" He reached up to grab her but was sluggish from the booze, and she broke away with a fearsome "No!" and rolled off him, turning her back to him, turning instead toward the college kid sleeping in the hollow.

A black adder within him constricted Mack's intestines, squeezing them tightly in its cold flesh, and Mack moaned aloud, rolled his head wildly, set bleary eyes on a dully gleaming object by his hand: his switchblade. She had opened it for him, laid it next to his hand.

He remembered.

MAURICE CARLOS RUFFIN holds an MFA from University of New Orleans. He is a member of Peauxdunque Writers Alliance and MelaNated Writers Collective. His work appears in the *Apalachee Review*, *Regarding Arts & Letters*, *Ellipsis*, and *Unfathomable City*, a New Orleans atlas (edited by Rebecca Solnit and published by the University of California). "The Pie Man," a short story appearing in the *South Carolina Review*, received the University of New Orleans Creative Writing Workshop's 2011 Ernest Svenson Fiction Award. His other awards include the 2013 Joanna Leake Prize for Fiction Thesis. Maurice is currently writing a novel.

HEROES AND VILLAINS

Ian hits his wife for the first time after watching a bootleg slasher movie on T.V. They're sitting on their two-toned loveseat when he notices Jaye staring at him, the soft glow of the television moonlighting her face. He reaches for a bag of kettle corn. She hasn't had any, although she used to love it. Instead she nurses a glass of bourbon. Her second of the last half hour. He's only had soda. He stops his leg from shaking, recalling that it makes Jaye think him afraid.

"Care for any?" Jaye shakes the glass of Bourbon at Ian. Something's wrong with the heating system and she says liquor keeps the chill from getting to her. Every day for the past several weeks, she's been on the sofa when he leaves for his nursing job at the hospital and when he returns. He worries she'll grow roots, that she'll lie there forever, forgetting the people who need her outside.

"No," he says. The coat rack near the front door is a scarecrow. Only Jaye's black, plastic-brimmed hat sits on top of it. He doesn't know where her badge or service revolver are. She might have thrown them out with the trash.

"What's eating you?" Since she's been on leave, Jaye wears socks on her hands for warmth.

Something thumps against the top of their apartment house. Ian glances up. Wind must have knocked loose the tarp, he imagines, leaving it to quiver like a blue flame. Hurricane Malecia was the worst storm to hit New Orleans since Hurricane Katrina when Ian was a teenager. Malecia didn't flood any of the houses in their neighborhood, but it cleaved a section of roof tiles away. A man was supposed to fix the hole last week, but he hasn't. A lot of people need his services.

"We both know you miss it," Ian says. Light from the television plays across Jaye's cheeks, turning her mahogany skin the color of Spanish moss. "You can go back tomorrow if you want."

"This is good." Bourbon trembles in her hand.

Near the end of their movie, a freak in a St. Bernard dog mask kills one of the main characters with a sledgehammer. He had been disguised as their friend. But that scene is over, and the survivors have escaped from the sewers into daylight and the city's futuristic skyscrapers after a week underground. People on the surface gape in revulsion as the survivors, coated in the filth of their misfortunes, approach. Ian scoops the last kernels of kettle corn into his mouth.

"You'll feel better," Ian says. "You can call your sergeant and tell him you're back to normal."

"Is that what I am?" Jaye pulls the hand socks off and rubs the diminishing scar on her upper arm. After the shooting, Ian cleaned and dressed her wound daily. It's healing, but she still has night terrors.

"You can put on your supersuit, and I'll drive you over in the morning."

Chief Compass gave Jaye a medal of valor following the incident. This was no surprise to Ian. She began collecting commendations as soon as she earned her commission five years ago. He sometimes called her a superhero, and referring to her police uniform as a supersuit always made her smile.

She doesn't smile now. Her mouth is a hyphen.

Ian caresses Jaye's bare knee, but the coldness of her skin sends a shudder up his arm. Their relationship has been in trouble for some time. No one's ever made the mistake of calling Ian brave or bold, and he is concerned that she may have finally become disgusted by this understanding of him. They haven't slept together in months.

Jaye tosses her socks onto the floor and stalks through the kitchen. By the time he reaches her, she's dead-bolted the bedroom door. He jiggles the knob.

"Go away," she says. "I'm so sick of watching your sick crap."

Ian has always loved horror films, especially where the villain gets the last word. Their first date was to a midnight screening of *Invasion of the Body Snatchers*. Ian had snuck them into the theater on Canal Street. Jaye had watched the movie through her fingers, her brown eyes sparkling in the light. Monsters terrified her. Ian found this endearing because she was a black belt in karate and could disable a person twice her size in one smooth motion.

Wisps of her dark hair had shimmered in that darkened theater. He'd wanted to touch the soft down and hold her, but when he'd reached out she caught his wrist in midair and squeezed so hard he yelped.

"I'm sorry," she'd said as she left the theater. Ian had found her outside by the marquis posters, one hand on her forehead, the other over her breast. She'd stiffened when she saw him. "I thought—"

"You thought I was going to hit you," he'd said. She nodded. The idea roiled his stomach. That he would hurt someone so beautiful, someone he was already taken by horrified him. "I'm not that kind of guy."

After a few minutes holed up in their bedroom, Jaye opens the door.

"You don't even have a real job." She leans against the doorjamb. "You change diapers all day. Don't tell me what to be."

Ian had wanted to be a pediatrician, but the thought of the intense competition he would find in medical school scared him off the idea.

"They need you—"

She slaps him, and the spark travels from his cheek to the back of his throat. He's reminded of his parents and their nightly scuffles, of the ugly scar on his chin his dad gave him, and, for some reason, of the first time Jaye demonstrated a straight-arm bar takedown on him. At the dojo where she trained, she pressed his face against the dirty linoleum. And Ian felt that was where he belonged.

"You should have joined up with your father," she says, still leaning against the door jamb, her arms crossing her breasts.

Ian freezes. He wants to stop her so that he can respond, but Jaye brushes past him into the hallway.

"At least he's a real man," she says.

Ian's face flushes. He turns toward the living room where the television light is flickering like a campfire. Of all the buttons she could push tonight, none stings so much as this. His dad, Luke, like all of the men in his family, is a low life. He and Ian's uncles were drunks and occasional burglars who masqueraded as a home improvement crew, looting dwellings for fun and profit. Luke had even tried to bring his son along a few times when Ian was a teenager, but Ian would freeze. One time, the sight of the victim's family portraits watching him, accusing him, stopped Ian in his tracks. He sat on the arm of their couch and pulled down one of their portraits.

"What are you?" Luke asked. "On vacation?" Ian knew that there was no right answer. Too many times a response had led to a backhand.

"Kid ain't made for this," Gabe had said, a TV set in his arms. "He's got yellow blood."

Gabe was Luke's strong man, could lift the back end of a small car from the ground while Luke stole the wheels.

When Luke ripped the portrait from Ian's hand that night, Ian had shielded his face with a forearm, but Luke dropped the frame to the beige carpet and crushed the glass under his heel.

Now, Ian often asks himself what Luke would do in a situation, and then does the opposite. This was why Ian chose medicine as a career. Luke never cared for anyone but himself. Still, Jaye admires Luke. Luke has spent almost half of his life in prison, going back in almost as soon as he got out each time, but Jaye once said that criminals like Luke at least have character. When they get caught, they take their licks like men and move on. Ian would do well to follow Luke's example.

When she passes Ian in the hallway, Jaye bops Ian's shoulder, and time jumps in his mind. Even as his fist connects twice with the side of her face, he sees his hands wrapped around her throat, his reddened thumbs pressing into her trachea. Jaye's tongue thrashes like wildfire.

Ian has never felt a rush like this: to be fully in control. The notion makes his stomach plummet. When he lets go, Jaye falls to the floor. Her cheek is darkening and the corners of her eyes run. Ian hears something like a growl.

"Is that all?" she says. "Jesus, you hit like a wet nurse."

Jaye pulls herself up and grabs the back of Ian's head. She bites his neck. He backs away, feeling for blood; he's afraid she will hit him. Instead, Jaye shoves him against the wall and unzips his jeans with one hand. Ian tries to block her hand. He doesn't know how angry she is or what she might do to him.

Her brown eyes blaze, and Ian recognizes the Jaye he hasn't seen in months. He reaches underneath her sweatshirt and feels the warm fabric of a bra cup.

Then he's inside her, and they are bound as if by rope.

* * *

Luke recently appeared at Ian's job, like an un-exorcised spirit. Law enforcement has been stationed around Women & Children's Hospital since the babies started dying. Two infants have died in the past three weeks; a four year old in the critical care ward too. All of the deaths were labeled questionable, which is another way of saying a killer is on the loose, but no one knows the who or even the how.

Angela, Ian's supervisor, says she doesn't know how long she can deal with all the death. She's been an infant nurse for over twenty years, and says that a person can only take so much gloom before it becomes too much. If someone like Angela, someone who twice won the National Nightingale Award for Excellence in Nursing before Malecia struck. … Ian's mind spun. If she can break down, what hope does he have?

Near the cafeteria doors, several deputies gather, hands propped against their utility belts. Ian tugs up the collar of his turtleneck. He wishes it was a hoodie. The hickey on the side of his neck throbs, feels as if he's growing a second head. And too, the back of his hand is too swollen to close completely. His knuckles are fuchsia. He'll have to find some pain meds if he's going to get any work done today. He won't be able take vitals or type his charts into the computer without usable fingers.

Luke laughs with the herd of deputies, seeming for all the world like he's on duty too. He nods. Ian doesn't acknowledge him. Luke had shown up a few days after Malecia, helping clear fallen tree limbs and other debris from the hospital entrance. He has a long rap sheet. Ian doesn't know how Luke conned the hospital into giving him a steady position, but he knows that Luke only came here as a way of exerting control over him. Luke has no one in his sphere of influence since Mama raised her hand and cursed him. When Ian reaches the elevator banks, he hears a voice.

"You can't keep running from me, kid." The voice is so close that it seems to come from within. The hairs on the back of Ian's neck stand up at the sound of his father's voice.

Luke faces Ian with his arms extended, as if he expects Ian to flee like a frightened child.

"Don't you remember we were like beans and rice before things got crazy?"

When Ian was little, Luke beat him any time he cried. He cried a lot. It was Luke who gave his son the nickname *Baby*. Ian never lets anyone call him that anymore. This was a matter of pride for Ian, a sign that he was a free adult, but Luke is a reminder that Baby is still alive.

"How long before you're arrested for stealing from the supply room?" Ian says.

"I saw your place took a hit from the storm," Luke says. "And I saw that thing in the paper about Jaye too."

"I don't want you lurking around here," Ian says.

"We're not so different," Luke says.

Ian and Luke are both light-skinned and sparrow-boned, but Luke's missing a chunk of flesh beneath his left cheekbone. It gives him a skeletal appearance. Ian wishes he was the one who had done it, but it was Mom. Mom was always willing to forgive Luke for what he did to them until the day she became unwilling.

"I've been studying the Tao," Luke says. "Trying to better myself. Yin yang and everything."

Ian checks the time on his cell phone, grimaces at his sore hand.

Luke punches the elevator button. "Fine. We don't have to talk about us, but how's my girl?"

Ian never saw his dad as happy as the day Ian married Jaye. Luke called her a girl who knew what she was and said she might add some steel to Ian's backbone. Ian still thinks Jaye's the only thing Luke has ever really liked about him, the one thing Ian got right. Ian doesn't disagree.

Luke grabs Ian's bruised hand before Ian can pull away. His dad's touch is soft, almost comforting. Luke lets go of Ian's hand.

"Like I said at your wedding." Luke partially rolls down Ian's collar and strokes the bandage covering his neck. "You caught a dragon when you found that one."

Ian pulls away. When the elevator dings its arrival, he scuttles into the compartment. He thinks Luke will follow him on. Is relieved when he doesn't.

"You still think you're better than me?" Luke gives Ian a Boy Scout salute as the doors clamp shut.

The elevator lurches upward, and Ian becomes aware of the rapid movement of his own chest. He's hyperventilating.

After getting a handful of Percocet from a co-worker in the pharmacy who owes him a favor, Ian enters his work area on the top floor of the hospital, stuffs cotton puffs and empty blood vials into his smock pocket. The pain in his hand is subsiding. Ian is the only male nurse in the NIC-U, the neonatal intensive care unit. Sometimes he thinks this should make him stronger than the women he works alongside. If only it were so.

He walks along the narrow aisle between incubators. It's a small unit now. There had been nearly thirty babies, but since the hurricane, many of the relatively healthy children were moved to the cities where their parents relocated. The seven remaining very sick babies, wrapped in pink or blue blankets, look like a carton of broken Easter eggs. Now there are only six, plus Pia Patin.

Pia is not Pia's real name. Ian gave it to her because he thought being nameless made her like a crab without a shell, vulnerable. The day after Malecia arrived seven weeks ago, Ian was part of a group of medical volunteers working out of Louis Armstrong Airport. Families rushed onto choppers and planes bound for points all across the U.S. Pia's parents, who were undocumented immigrants and feared deportation, didn't want to leave the newborn. Pia had nearly drowned in oil-contaminated floodwater, but Ian assured them that she was in good hands. He was wrong. Everyone, including Pia's parents, thought Pia would be flown in a separate medical transport to Oklahoma City where a crisis team waited, but after Pia's parents left for Oklahoma, the triage doctors said she was too sick to travel. In the confusion, her parents' contact information was lost and Pia was brought here without their knowledge. No one has heard from the parents.

Pia's dark-eyed, like Jaye, and wearing only a flimsy diaper. The plastic crib is tied to a machine of canisters and tubes; the tubes crawl over the crib rim and into Pia's chest, arms and mouth. She looks as if she's being eaten by a Portuguese Man of War.

The machine is supposed to make her stronger, but her lung capacity has decreased sharply in the past forty-eight hours. Ian wonders if God is trying to siphon back the shot of life he gave her. It may be for the best. Most of these babies won't live long enough to ride a tricycle. Those that do will live short, painful lives.

Jaye's face. The shock on her face after Ian punched her echoes through his mind. Before he left that morning, he watched her swallow a few aspirins. The blow left a welt on her cheek, and there were faint medallions on her throat where he grabbed her. She didn't mention any of it.

"Nurse Villariago," Angela, the charge nurse, says. She has crow's feet that look the same whether she's laughing or frowning. "We don't stare at the children. We treat them."

"Sorry," Ian says.

"What's all this?" Angela gestures at Ian's wounds. "You're not the one are you? The maniac?"

Pia is silent in her crib. Ian isn't sure if Angela is serious.

* * *

Five days after the first beating, the shadows outside of Ian and Jaye's window come alive. It's two a.m., and Ian is staring at the ceiling as Jaye sleeps next to him. She rolls toward him and groans. Her face is distorted by shadow. Their bedroom is on the second floor of the townhouse and sits at the head of a tall evergreen, the fingers and forearms of which spread across the window panes. A ripping sound comes from the roof and something crashes below the window. Ian smells Bourbon and peppercorns. He imagines the tree digits stretching onto the bed and squeezing the life out of them. Jaye screams.

The sketchy police department incident report and an all-too-brief newspaper article painted a clumsy picture of what had happened to Jaye during the hurricane. Like something one of the palsied adolescents on the extended care unit might have drawn and colored in pastels.

On September 20th, six days after Malecia, Jaye and her partner and mentor, Detective Ben Parker, had arrived at a nursing home on New Orleans' East Side. The area had not flooded, but the residents were in bad shape, having run out of provisions. The back-up generator had failed during the humid day before, and one woman was in a heat-stroke-induced coma. Three armed men had appeared at the gate to the nursing home, and shots were fired. When Ben and Jaye arrived, Ben chased the men to a junk yard behind the building. On Ben's orders Jaye had remained behind to secure the residents, a decision she would immediately regret. When she went in search of her partner, one of the attackers shot Jaye in the arm, but she chased the men away. Eventually, she found Mitch face down in a ditch filled with hubcaps. He'd only fallen three feet, but that was enough to break his neck and kill him.

* * *

Jaye leaps from the bed, naked as a flame, and snatches the bedspread, uncovering Ian.

"You're worthless." Jaye throws the laughing monkey figurine from the nightstand at Ian.

Luke had given it to them along with the *see no evil* and *speak no evil* monkeys as wedding gifts. The figurine hits the headboard, and Ian is showered with fragments. He tastes blood. His lip is busted. He jumps to his feet, arms and hands outstretched in a defensive posture.

Jaye's father beat her too, but her reaction was to join the force as an adult and become a protector. No matter what, Ian tells himself, he won't hurt her again. She can roundhouse-kick him out of the window, but he will not become Luke.

She shoves Ian, but he doesn't move. She pushes again, and he trips, banging his head on the high dresser. When he's on all fours, a glint catches his eye. Her badge. He grabs it and climbs to his feet.

"You're going back," he says.

She smiles.

Jaye snatches the badge from him and jams it into his face. Ian realizes that both this time and last, she didn't use any of her fighting skills against him. Nothing she learned at the academy. Nothing from the dojo. If Jaye wanted to, she could have knocked him out, hog-tied him and had her police friends finish him off in an abandoned warehouse.

"What's the matter?" Jaye pauses. "You're not crying are you?"

He is. So is Jaye.

"I know you want to hit back," she says. "Hit me."

Ian balls his fist, but he doesn't punch.

* * *

The next morning Ian goes looking for Luke around the cafeteria and doesn't see him. That's fine with Ian. Most people in the halls are hurrying toward the ambulance bay. A young couple runs past him. He yells for them to stop. They don't, but it's clear they recognize him too. He follows them.

"They caught the baby-killer," an orderly says when they reach the rear entrance of the hospital. Ian self-consciously shields his forehead, which has a pulsing, fuchsia welt from last night. Dozens of people have gathered in the ambulance bay as if for a parade. Police cars and a large security van are parked just beyond the portico. Officers with walkie-talkies and shotguns guard the area. The officers warn the crowd to keep their distance. A chill runs through Ian. If Luke were somehow responsible for the infant deaths, what would that say about Ian? Was Ian capable of doing such a thing?

"You took care of Ada." The woman of the couple rubs Ian's shoulder. She has a heavy accent, but Ian understands. "Thank you."

Ada. Pia's real name. Her parents found their child. Ada's father says, more in gestures than in words, that someone stumbled onto the murderer hovering over Ada's crib.

"That's her," Ada's mother says, pointing. The crowd parts as several men lead Angela out of the hospital. Her wrists are handcuffed behind her back. She looks directly at Ian as the officers drag her by.

"But who caught her?" Ian says.

Ada's mother points again. At the far end of the invisible string streaming from the tip of her finger, through the middle of a group of policemen in windbreakers, and to a man rubbing the back of his neck is Luke, who is gesturing back toward the hospital. It was Luke, searching for Ian, who had spotted Angela through the observation glass. He found Angela preparing to inject a syringe full of air into the child's fragile arm.

Ian doesn't know what to say to Luke. None of this will change their relationship. Luke will always be a scumbag, but Ian can't help but ask a question. Luke might have an answer.

"Why would she do that to those babies?" Ian says.

Luke rubs his chin and shrugs.

* * *

When Ian arrives home late that evening, the house is as they left it the previous night. In the kitchen, the transom window to their bedroom is shattered, and the refrigerator is overturned. Clothes that were pulled out of the drawers are strewn on the kitchen floor like seaweed and peppered with shards from the figurines and flower pots they smashed. Ian did not hit Jaye last night. However, he had tossed a vase through the living room television screen. Jaye cleared the wet bar with a broom handle. One thing led to another and they had sex on the bar, against the wall, and a third time on the floor.

Ian knows it's not over. He'll have to prod Jaye until she wakes up from her dark fantasy. He wonders if Luke had thought he was prodding Ian and his mother all those years ago.

But as Ian enters their bedroom, he finds Jaye standing at the full-length mirror, which, somehow, was not damaged. She's dressed in her complete uniform, hat on head, revolver and baton slung low across her hips. Her sky blue button-down shirt is pressed, and her badge shines as if sunlit.

"I don't want to," she says. "But I need to."

She unclasps her revolver, and Ian backs away. But Jaye doesn't grab the gun. She rubs his chin and kisses him.

"I don't know if I can come back to you after this." She examines his hand, which has turned dark as an eggplant since he hit her.

"I shouldn't have let this happen," Ian says.

"This is what we made."

Ian doesn't move. Her footfalls travel down the steps and out the front door. The car engine starts, and gravel pings against the side of the house as Jaye speeds into the night.

Luke knocks on Ian's door at daybreak. He's placed a ladder and box of tiles near the foot of the steps that lead into the house. A hammer juts out of his coverall pocket.

"I'm here to fix the hole in the roof," he says.

The blue tarp is on the grass, tangled in a weathervane.

"But I never told you about it," Ian says.

"She did."

Ian invites Luke inside.

At midday, Luke finishes fastening the last of the tiles to the roof. He gives Ian a lighter, and Ian piles the tarp and tiles in the driveway and burns them all. More smoke than flame.

LORETTA DIANE WALKER is a two-time Pushcart nominee and an award-winning poet. She has published two collections of poetry and her work appears in numerous publications. Her manuscript *Word Ghetto* won the 2011 Bluelight Press Book Award (1st World Publishing Press, 2011). She teaches music at Reagan Magnet School in Odessa, Texas. Loretta received a BME from Texas Tech University and earned a MA from The University of Texas of the Permian Basin.

HOW TO FIGHT LIKE A GIRL

To fight like a girl
you must first become an ocean
to hold the crush of tears
pooling beneath the ducts.

You must learn to walk
through the day with a fish of fear
floating through
the coral of your belly.

At the sound of battle,
you must paint your nails
the boldest blood shade of red
and use them like shark teeth
to maim and masticate
those piranha emotions
gnawing at your strength.

You must get off your knees
after the tentacles of cancer and chemo,
nausea and fatigue, pain and weakness
grasp your body and feed on all things woman.

You must remember you are a woman
when lavas of sweat roll from your bald head
and flank your face, and your lips crack and flake
like a dried beach.

You must stand straight, wash yourself in softness,

tattoo stars on your fists and sing praises
for the half-moons in the sky of your breasts.

A LETTER TO THE WOMAN IN THE BLACK DRESS STANDING NEAR THE WINDOW

I don't know how to transpose the music of quails,
interpret the language of goats,
or use words to draw the expression on your face.
It's not loneliness; loneliness is round like a hole
waiting to be filled with mud thick darkness
or emptiness so deep it echoes.
It's not peace; peace is a rectangle
stretched on a canvas with the silhouette of winter
napping on the front porch.
The snow is orderly, perfectly shaped to induce tranquility.
Your face is a square, a delicate field
irrigated with rows and rows of questions.

What is stilling your body,
fixing your eyes like an owl's?

Outside my window the wind is tiptoeing,
rummaging through a couple of battered pines—
searching the archives of its branches for artifacts,
dropping pinecones and sparrow feathers.
Its long hair is tangled in the string of wind chimes;
they betray it with their soft ding. ding. ding.

Lady, your black dress is a distraction,
the hem barely legal over the trunk of your thighs.
It, like you, roars for attention.
Did you read the sign above your head?

Quiet please. Let others enjoy the silence.
How can we when the earth is constantly whispering?
Only the deaf know silence.

www.ingramcontent.com/pod-product-compliance
Lightning Source LLC
Chambersburg PA
CBHW071955170626
46813CB00005B/1885